"Destiny is not a matter

This famous quote by Williams Jenning Bryan has never been truer than in the life journey of Lana Portnoy. Lana's story offers encouragement and challenge that will inspire all who read her transparent revealing of her joys and pains. I am grateful to count Lana Portnoy as a dear friend, having the honor of serving as her pastor at Calvary Orlando Church for the better part of a decade.

Those of us who are blessed to have Lana's journey intersect with our own quickly discover that she is one of the most genuine people we know. Her very real love for people and focused devotion to her Savior are readily apparent. Lana's love for people fuels her willingness to share both her victories and defeats with an amazing level of honesty. This book is a vivid expression of her love for God and for you!

My prayer is that God uses Lana's story to challenge yours. I am confident that as you read this incredible book you will hear "Destiny is not a matter of chance, it is a matter of choice" echoed in each chapter. The Missing Piece *is a wonderful guide to the most important choice. May you discover the missing piece and make a choice for Destiny!*

Blessings,
Edwin Garvin

THE MISSING PIECE

Finding the Hidden Hand of God in Your Life

LANA PORTNOY

The Missing Piece
Finding The Hidden Hand of God in Your Life
by Lana Portnoy

Published by:

HigherLife Development Services, Inc.
PO Box 622307
Oviedo, FL 32762
(407) 563-4806
ahigherlife.com

ISBN: 978-1-951492-56-4 Paperback

ISBN: 978-1-951492-57-1 eBook

Printed in the United States of America

TABLE OF CONTENTS

FOREWORD

I have known Lana and Barry Portnoy for nearly three decades, and over that time we have grown from co-laborers in ministry to family. I have heard bits and pieces of their individual and 'corporate' stories during our many travels and some "family time," but it wasn't until I read their entire story all in the same sitting that I felt the impact of the immense pressure and amazing victories that their life's story has to offer. You might ask, "What will I gain by reading this book?" Please read on.

As I read this manuscript, I found myself constantly asking the question, "How do you handle such unusual emotional and spiritual pressure," and "How would I respond if I was dealt that same deck of cards?" I often found myself shaking my head in disbelief at the frequency of heart-breaking tragedies, and just as often found myself marveling at the personal responses to some potentially life-threatening experiences. Yes, some of the pain might be classified as "self-induced," but then there's all the rest of life as well. Over my more than forty years of pastoral ministry I can assure you that many souls never fully recover from half of what you will read in these pages. I have seen a t-shirt with a saying that becomes more and more relevant as the years go by. It reads: "Life is not for wimps!"

Apart from the many situations that Lana and Barry have faced that make this book much more than simply a retelling of their journey, is the final chapter that outlines and highlights "lessons learned." You have heard it said, I am certain, that if we forget the lessons of the past, we are destined to repeat them. Lana has infused this book with powerful life lessons that are supported and highlighted with scripture to hold fast when encountering the bumps and bruises that life often presents. No formulas here for an "easy fix," just some good solid help for handling the road when it gets rough and long.

I have spent many years in pastoral as well as traveling worship ministry; nearly forty-five to date. When asked what it's all about, I sometimes answer folks that "I am simply trying to help people 'do life.'" When you read your Bible through the eyes of "family" you come away with a very different perspective, I believe. Barry and Lana have become family to me and my household. We have walked together for decades, I know them, love and deeply respect them for who they are as much as what they do. I believe the reason Lana wrote this book was to help others "do life" through the tough lessons learned in the school of hard knocks. I am certain you will be encouraged and even challenged by reading and considering the wise words shared with you here.

Paul Wilbur
Worship Artist/Pastor
Celebration Church

INTRODUCTION

THE GOD FACTOR

Jewish wisdom imparts:

"Train up a child in the way he should go,
And when he is old he will not depart from it."[1]
Good people leave an inheritance to their children's children.

The Old Testament Scriptures (for Jews, the *Tanach*), place a high premium on Jewish parents teaching their children about the Living God of Abraham, Isaac, and Jacob. The spiritual inheritance we give to our children can bear fruit and impact our families for generations. Teaching and training your children about the Living God who created them in His image and who loves them is the most important inheritance and legacy parents can hand down to their children.

I was born in Northeastern Pennsylvania in 1940. My father was a (CPA) Certified Public Accountant, a graduate of the University of Pennsylvania. He had a private practice but also taught accountants the courses they needed to pass the CPA exam. He was a guest speaker on several occasions at accounting conventions. My loving mother raised her five children and did some volunteer work. She was raised Catholic and my father was Jewish. Our parents made the decision that we would be raised in the Jewish faith. Much like Ruth's commitment to Naomi, my mother followed her husband's Jewish faith. She went with us to Temple and served in the sisterhood. However, she never converted to Judaism.

We attended and were members of a reformed Temple. My grandfather was one of the original founders of the Temple. I loved being raised in the Jewish faith. I attended many youth conferences and was a counselor at the Jewish Community Center day camp. I am convinced without this religious upbringing I would not have had any knowledge of God. My gratitude is limitless in being forever thankful to my parents for all the good things they imparted to us, especially **the God Factor**.

I am inviting you to go on a journey with me from childhood through today as a woman who knew about God and discovered an intimacy with Him that brought amazing love, joy, and peace into my life, marriage and family.

A journey of faith in our Loving God doesn't start with an *instant* intimacy. Such a relationship grows…it's a process.

Along the way, there are mountain tops and valleys, highs and lows, along with failures and victories. I have been amazed at all the miracles and amazing truths that God has brought my way from such a humble beginning as a Jewish girl. I now know that the hidden hand of God guided me in the ways He desired to bless and mature me. As history's greatest Jewish missionary for the Messiah wrote: "God is at work in all things for the good of those who love Him and are called according to His purposes."[2]

I encourage you to read my story straight through and then to go back to the beginning of my story and study the God Factor principles uncovered in each chapter.

"Hear, O Israel: The LORD our God, the LORD is one! You shall love the LORD your God with all your heart, with all your soul, and with all your strength." [3]

I am Jewish by birth. My Jewish heritage instilled in me as a child has become part of my spiritual identity as a believer, one who declares Jesus (Yeshua) as Messiah—the Anointed One of God. At the core of my being, my every breath is filled with a song of praise, my every act is one of worship, and my every desire is to love God my true Father with all my heart, soul, and strength. Of course, this is the first and greatest commandment and the second is like it, "Love your neighbor as yourself."

You can uncover and apply these God Factors in your own

life, learn from my mistakes and successes, apply Scriptural truths to deepen your relationships with God and others, and finally experience an intimacy with God that will move you from knowing about Him to deeply loving Him, others, and yourself. Read on….

CHAPTER 1

THE FAMILY FACTOR

My mother was a very compassionate person who loved raising her children. In the early years my mother was alone taking care of her four children, because my father was in the Midwest serving in the army. I am certain that my mother had her hands full. My brother and sisters who were older, got the measles. A short time later, they all came down with the chicken pox. My sister Sandy who was two years older than me got rheumatic fever and had to be on total bed rest. The first memory I have of my father was when he came home from the army. One day, I was picked up at school and told that our father was home. The next day we moved across town into a much bigger house which we grew up in. It was a lovely house with so many rooms and a big backyard for us to play in. There was a big tennis court behind our house where my father and his friends played tennis. In the winter my parents would hose down the tennis court so it would freeze over and make ice. Then the brownie and girl scout troops that my mother was involved with would come over and ice skate.

My father's place in the family was one of honor and he was a very good provider. However, because of the way he was raised, he was a strong believer in discipline, and he had strict rules we were expected to follow without question. He came from a family who were all high academic achievers and he had very little patience with us. He often criticized us and told us we were dumb. We could never seem to measure up to his impossible high standards. As a result, we passed, but never were honor roll students. My sister Penny, who was eleven years younger, excelled in school because she didn't receive this verbal abuse.

In spite of the negative side of our family dynamics, I realize now there are no perfect families and I do have many wonderful memories of growing up. My sisters and I went to Girl Scout Camp in the beautiful Poconos in Pennsylvania. We also went to Atlantic City where my father rented a house for the summer near the beach. My parents always displayed a generous heart by the way they lived and the goodness they showed to others. My impression of childhood is that I was blessed to grow up in a time when life was good, simple, and wholesome. The smallest things brought us pleasure. Going swimming, riding bikes, playing marbles, skating, bowling, or going to the movie theater were all fun.

When I was about eight years old, our family doctor discovered I had a heart murmur. In those days, fear of overexertion caused my parents to put me on bed rest for a while. Thankfully, my doctors and parents later decided some activity would strengthen my heart. My mother decided to enroll me in dancing lessons. Little did I know that dance would become such a big part of my life.

"Write these commandments that I've given you today on your hearts. Get them inside of you and then get them inside your children. Talk about them wherever you are, sitting at home or walking in the street; talk about them from the time you get up in the morning to when you fall into bed at night. Tie them on your hands and foreheads as a reminder inscribe them on the door-posts of your homes and on your city gates."[4]

This God Factor was initiated by my parents, perhaps unwittingly, but nevertheless the truth that God was real and active in my life began to shape within me and empower my talents and gifts. The arts of dance and later music were inspired by the One who made me and gave me the desire and ability to worship and praise Him. My story will reveal how God was the hidden actor and invisible scribe in writing the *narrative of me.*

While my parents were far from perfect reflections of God, they sowed into me a Jewish seed which would take root and bear wonderful fruit years later in my life. More about this later….

Dance, Dance, Dance

Throughout the rest of my school years, I took dancing lessons. I was in many recitals, talent shows, and the Children's Hour TV show in Philadelphia. My mother became a bit of a stage mom.

She scheduled my practice, dance lessons, and public appearances.

Near the end of my senior year in high school, my mother arranged an audition for me at Juilliard School of Music in New York City. They had a highly rated dance department that she felt would move my dancing career forward. I remember feeling very nervous, especially after I found out my father was going to the audition with us. The audition was a disaster, I knew I was not qualified as I watched the other dancers. They were highly trained in ballet and I was not. The faculty spoke to my parents and said I had great musicality and they saw potential in me.

My parents took their advice and sent me to the Jacob's Pillow Dance Festival in Massachusetts for the summer. Because I was leaving for this dance festival, I didn't get to walk with my classmates at my own high school graduation. Instead, I went to a famous dance camp where I had dance classes all day during the week and performances to attend on the weekend. This kind of training was totally different than my fun days as a younger girl. This hard work was new to me. The ballet classes I took every day helped me to become a stronger dancer.

At the end of the summer, I went back to Juilliard for my second audition. Because I was prepared for this audition, it went much better. The faculty were pleased with my progress and they accepted me into their dance program. My parents were happy. They expected me to work hard, practice, and excel at dance.

For the first time in my life,
I felt I had my father's approval.

My earthly father's love was conditional. I had to work hard to earn his love. My Heavenly Father would teach me over the years that His love (in Greek called *agape*) was unconditional.

I started Juilliard in September of 1957. While I was in school, I met many extraordinary and talented dancers, musicians, and opera singers of the highest caliber. Most of the dancers in my class came from the famous High School of the Performing Arts in New York City. They had years of experience and great training which I didn't have. The first year was very exciting but it was also the hardest. I was behind the others in my class however I learned to work hard and persevere. We had excellent ballet teachers, but it was my modern dance classes that I really loved. Our modern dance teachers were all professional dancers who danced at one time or another with the famous Martha Graham Dance Company. They were very strong dancers and the choreography was unique and beautiful in every way.

The first year was very exciting but it was also the hardest.

I was a naïve small-town girl, just seventeen years old, and I had to learn how to live in the city. I was stressed on a daily basis and had some very challenging times. I lived downtown and one of my biggest problems was going to school on the subway. Because I didn't know the subway system, I had to ask people which train I should take. Many times, I was given the wrong directions. One day, I ended up lost somewhere in Brooklyn. Another time, I was in the Bronx and I was always late for class. After a few weeks, the school administrator called my parents and strongly suggested I move somewhere near the school. This move certainly made my life much easier.

Another time, I was walking down the street and a young man came over to me and started talking to me. A taxi driver yelled at me and said, "Lady you just got robbed." I quickly looked down at my purse which was now open and saw my wallet was gone, so was the young man. The lesson I learned was not to talk to strangers.

It took a while, but in time I gained confidence and became a "city girl" who knew her way around. During this time, I also learned the value of hard work.

I asked some of the Jewish girls who lived in New York if I could go with them to their Temple or Synagogue services. They looked at me as if I had asked something strange and said, "We don't attend Temple services. We only go once a year on the High Holy Days." That surprised me, but I decided this was not my concern.

CHAPTER 2

THE MARRIAGE FACTOR

My First Love

In the summer of 1958, I took a job as the dance instructor for an exclusive Jewish camp in upstate New York. The campgrounds were breathtakingly beautiful, and I always loved working with young people. Every night, the counselors had time off and we got together to dance.

The first night, I met a nice young man who danced with me all night. Afterwards, he was kind enough to walk me back to my cabin. He was a gentle person with good communication skills who loved my artistry and I loved his intelligence. A New York native, this new boyfriend attended college in North Carolina. How humorous it was to me that the teenage girls in my cabin said I got the cutest guy in the camp.

Some nights, we would sit out in the fields and talk for hours. He was the sweetest man I had ever met. I found myself falling in love with him over the summer and I was sure he had the same feelings for me. What made it even more special is the fact that this was the first time I was in love. The summer was now winding down and we were all getting ready to go home. I found it hard to say goodbye the last night we were together. He asked if he could write to me. Of course, I said yes. This made our goodbye a little easier knowing we were going to stay in touch.

He came to see me in Pennsylvania, met my family, and we had a great time together. We continued to keep in touch and in early September, I went to New York to get ready for school. We took every chance we could to see each other. We both started school and wrote letters to each other every week. His letters were very beautiful. I should have known they would be because he had writing gifts and he loved literature. We saw each other often over the holidays. However, after New Year's Eve, he broke up with me. He said he had many years of college and law school ahead of him and he thought it would be best if we broke up. In silence, he drove me back to my apartment in Manhattan and all I can say is, I was heartbroken.

Life Changes

Three months after this very painful breakup I had an unexpected, uninvited, visitor from New York. It was a young man I knew from school. We had dated only two times in my first year at Juilliard. I was impressed with his great talent, but not with him. On our first date he took me to see a monster movie called Godzilla. At that time, I was not interested in him. He kept calling me and I just ignored him. One day, he showed up at my parents' house in Pennsylvania. He told me he heard my boyfriend and I had broken up and he wanted to start dating me. He totally won my parents over with his charm and great talent. He was a brilliant concert pianist who played Rhapsody in Blue with Paul Whiteman at Carnegie Hall when he was very young. He also was the piano soloist with different Philharmonic orchestras in several places in the United States. His brilliance and acclaim won him a full scholarship to Julliard School of Music. My father loved classical music, so naturally, he was very impressed.

To be honest, I was annoyed. I really did not know him well and I was still in love with my former boyfriend. I was depressed and after many months, I went out with him. He kept showing up at my parents' house and he was relentless! One day, he convinced my mother to go with him and help him pick out an engagement ring for me. After he proposed to me, I told my mother I didn't love him. She said it doesn't matter, he loves you and he will take care of you. My parents really loved him, so I finally said yes to his proposal.

After he proposed to me, I told my mother I didn't love him.

We were planning to get married in the Fall and my mother was planning a big Jewish wedding. He changed the plan and decided we should skip the formal wedding that every girl dreams of. He wanted to get married quickly so we could be together for the summer. In July of 1959, we got married in our Temple by our rabbi. The wedding was very small with only a few family members. There was no bride in a beautiful wedding gown, and nothing resembled the wedding I would have wanted. I was only nineteen years old. We had a two-day honeymoon because he had a summer job in Monticello, New York where he played with the orchestra in a large hotel. He arranged for me to get the job of running their day camp. Throughout the summer he worked until late at night, and I worked all day with children of all ages who wore me out. Like two ships passing in the night, we hardly saw each other. Everything revolved around him and his career. I honestly felt like I was married to a total stranger. We had very little communication and I was sorry I married him.

When the summer was over, we moved into our apartment by the school. The school year started and within a few months, I was extremely tired, and I was not feeling well. I was forcing myself to go to class, but I could not dance because I had developed severe abdominal pain. When I called home and explained to my mother what I was experiencing, she told us to come home right away. I ended up in the hospital in Pennsylvania with a cyst on my ovary that had ruptured, and I was bleeding internally. They removed one of my ovaries. Thank God I went home when I did.

Our family doctor told my parents I could not stay in school.

I was exhausted, anemic from the blood loss, and had lost a lot of weight. He said the dance program was too strenuous for me. When my parents told me, I had to drop out of school, I'm ashamed to say that I felt relief. I felt like an enormous weight had lifted. I do love and appreciate the art of dance even to this day, but it was not what I loved. I was tired of working so hard to be someone everyone else wanted me to be.

You only live one life.
Find your passion and the gifting that God gives you.
It will not be a burden, but something that you love.
Let God develop the gift in you.

Noted author and pastor, Joel Osteen writes, "I believe that God has put gifts and talents and ability on the inside of every one of us. When you develop that and you believe in yourself and you believe that you're a person of influence and a person of purpose, I believe you can rise up out of any situation."[5]

During this season of my life, I did not see what God was doing in me and through me. However, I found that the God given gift in me was music. Yes, music was the thing I had loved all my life and would become a primary way that I worshipped and praised Him.

From the time I was a child, I always heard music in my head. I sang in a trio in junior high school and I made the advanced chorus in high school. Now that I was no longer going to Juilliard, I started to sing with my husband's band. I loved music and I had on-the-job training. There were some hours of practice, but it was exciting, and I never felt like it was a burden. I worked with some of the finest musicians in the business.

After my husband graduated with a master's degree from Juilliard, he joined the Army. He auditioned for the concert band at the military academy at West Point, New York and was accepted. After basic training, we moved to West Point and spent seven years of our marriage there. He played with the large concert band and accompanied the West Point glee club. An officer's wife and I taught ballroom dance lessons at some private military schools in the area. I also taught ballet part time at a local dance studio.

I sang on weekends with small bands who played for the officers' club and the non-officers' club. I was the singer with the West Point big dance band. We played for all the cadet hops (dances) and I loved being the singer with this big dance band. It was truly a great honor to work with these fine musicians.

As my journey with God unfolds, you will learn how He instructed me in His ways for using the gifts and talents He gave me. I hope you will discover what He has imparted to you which will not only be a blessing to you but also to others as well. My story continues with some hard lessons to be learned about marriage, being a wife, and a parent.

Our two beautiful children were born in the army hospital at West Point. I remember my husband drove me to the hospital and told me to get out of the car and go have the baby. A woman came over to me with a wheelchair and helped me get into the hospital. My husband drove off to teach piano lessons. I was frightened and left alone and within a few hours gave birth to our beautiful daughter who we named Susan. She was a gift from God as all children are. I remember staying up all night thanking God for her and how beautiful she was. In this army hospital, you had to take care of your own baby. Two years later, I gave birth to our son and we named him Darren. He had auburn hair and I knew he was going to be tall.

I bought a Madam Alexander doll of Israel before Susan was born. The doll had dark hair and beautiful blue eyes and was dressed in an Israeli dress with a star of David on her neck. She was a collector doll and Susan had this doll on a shelf all her life. There is a reason I am telling you about this particular doll. We will leave her on the shelf for now and I will share it with you much later as she fits into the narrative of my story.

My life was busy raising children, singing, and teaching dancing lessons. I was greatly disappointed to find out my husband was a Jew in name only; he was an atheist. Things went from bad to worse. I struggled in this marriage for years and began to suffer with severe migraine headaches. They were so bad, I had to go to the hospital and get shots to be able to function. My husband was constantly criticizing and embarrassing me in front of other people, even when we were on stage. He had pictures of himself and famous people he played for on our walls. I had a hard time dealing with his self-centered and egotistical personality. He was never a loving husband or a practicing Jew. A fact he hid from me and my family even as we were getting married in a Jewish Temple by our rabbi.

My husband was an only child and he came from a broken home. I came from a large family. This made a big difference in how we viewed our husband and wife relationship. I was raised with love and some criticism from my dad, but my parents were both very generous and good people. We were taught to share and think of others not just ourselves. My husband and I grew further apart as the arguments and tension increased. After nine years in this unhealthy marriage, I filed for a divorce. No one in my family had ever gotten a divorce. My father was not happy with me to say the least; I divorced his favorite son-in-law. We worked out the legal arrangements which included child support and visiting rights. After our divorce, I never had another migraine.

I stayed in the upstate New York area and continued to work in a posh supper club as their singer. The musicians in the band were people I knew and had worked with before. I especially loved this job because I only had to work on the weekends. The children and I adjusted to our new life and were doing well. My ex-husband went on the road with the Guy Lombardo orchestra. He paid his child support, but the children did not get to see him very often.

My ex-husband apparently stayed in contact with some of my family members. He found out a favorite aunt of mine was sick with cancer and dying. He convinced her to change her will and take me out of it because I had divorced him. Guess who got my inheritance? Yes, he did. The worst part of this story is he never told me my aunt was dying. My heart ached to see her once again, but I never had the chance to say goodbye. He hid the money he received from her estate by buying land that he put in his new wife's name. Years later, she divorced him and sold the land that rightly belonged to me and my children. This was all very hurtful to me and it took me sometime before I could forgive him. God's Word tells us we have to forgive, and I did.

Forgiveness does not excuse their behavior.
Forgiveness prevents their behavior from destroying your heart.

My Second Love

About a year after my divorce, two friends introduced me to a handsome, divorced, Jewish man with two children. He called me several times and we started to date. I fell head over heels in love with him. He was kind and thoughtful and was a communicator. He was educated and had a good job, but what I loved the most about him was he was a practicing Jew. At that time, I was teaching ballet to children at the Jewish Community Center. I was also singing with a band on weekends at a posh supper club on the Hudson River. We dated for a year and then had a summer wedding. Our four children were in our small wedding. It was intimate and beautiful and this time, we had a real honeymoon.

We rented an apartment big enough for my two children and his two children who visited us every other weekend. Our children were about the same ages and they did well together. We were a happy Jewish couple, and this was the life I wanted. I gladly gave up the night club job to stay home and be a wife and mother.

About five months later, my husband came home early and told me he lost his job and he was depressed. He said we had to give up the apartment and move either into his mother's house or I could go home to Pennsylvania until he found another job. I decided to go home and stay with my older sister Rae and her family. I knew this was only a temporary situation and my children would be happier there than living with his mother who they really didn't know.

My husband kept in touch with me, but we lived apart for about five months. He was finding it difficult to find another job. Finally, he came to Pennsylvania to see us and said he had good news. He had taken a job in New Jersey working for his uncle. He went ahead of us and bought a house. He started work and the children and I came with the moving van to our new home in New Jersey.

The movers had just left our house when suddenly, I felt a severe stabbing pain across my chest. I thought I was having a heart attack because the pain was so bad. I had a hard time breathing and I was home alone with the children. I sent my daughter next door to get a neighbor, whom we had never met, to help us. Thank God that neighbor came over and called an ambulance. I called my husband and he came home immediately. I ended up in the hospital with pleurisy, pneumonia, and mononucleosis.

I cried out to God asking Him what is wrong?

I heard, "Get up and go far away and don't look back."

I went home from the hospital, took my medicines, and rested for several weeks. My husband told me he was sinking into another bad depression. He asked me to leave because he didn't want me to see him in this condition. We both cried, we had only been married less than a year. This was a heartbreak for both of us and another failed marriage for me. Our love story ended too soon.

I was sick in my body and my emotions.

A few weeks later, I called the movers and put my furniture in storage. I called my sister Sandy who lived in upstate New York. She said the children and I could come and stay with her until we knew what we wanted to do next. We visited her for a few days, and she said you can't stay in this area. You have too many memories here.

Then she said firmly, "*You have to go far away and don't look back.*"

That was the second time I heard this!

Then she said, "Let's go to Florida. You always wanted to go to Florida."

I don't know where she got that from. I never remember wanting to live in Florida. The truth is I was so tired and empty, I was willing to go wherever she suggested. We drove to Pennsylvania to say goodbye to our family. I remember my father calling us the wandering Jews. They were worried about me and the children, but I assured them I would stay in touch. My sister had a friend who told her we should go to the Orlando area as it would be a good place to raise my children. We drove two cars all the way to Orlando and did not get lost. That was truly amazing as there were no cell phones or GPS back then.

This was February of 1971. The trip was an absolute blur to me, but I vividly remember driving into Orlando on I–4. I had the windows down and I could smell the beautiful fragrance of orange blossoms. There were miles and miles of orange groves on both sides of the highway. It was warm and the sun was shining so bright. What a sharp contrast to the cold winter weather we had just left behind only days before. I remember feeling a sense of new beginnings. We stayed at a hotel for one night and I looked through the phone book to see if there was a Jewish community in the area. I was relieved to find out that there was. The next day we found and rented an apartment in a good school district, rented some furniture, and enrolled the children in school.

The next night, I got dressed up and went to find a singing job. I stopped at a gas station and asked the attendant where the live bands were playing. He said right around the corner there was a restaurant/nightclub with a very good band that got big crowds every night. I went there and introduced myself to the band leader, who said I could sing a few songs with them. This was a six-piece band and the musicians were all very good. The next day they called me and said I was hired, but their plan was to let the guitarist go. I knew he was a father of four or five children, so I turned down the job. The following day they called me and said I was hired, and they would keep the guitarist. I accepted the job offer and started work that week. They were a top-forty band and this style of music was different for me, but I was thankful for the work.

For about two years, my ex-husband had stopped paying me any child support, so it was imperative that I work. Later, when I did go to court for child support, I was awarded a pittance of $14.00 per week for each child. My ex-husband lied about his finances and it seemed there was nothing more I could do.

This new job was six nights a week and we also rehearsed some afternoons. When my sister had to leave, I hired a babysitter agency to watch my children. They were my prized possession and I wanted them to be safe. We all missed my sister, but I was grateful for all her help in getting us settled.

Working the night hours six nights a week was very hard on me. I got home late, and I had to get up early to get the children off to school. After they left, I went back to sleep.

I loved that I was able to be home with them after school. They did their homework and we had a nice dinner together before I had to go to work. I always told my children they were smart, and they were going to go to college. They had to work hard to be on the honor roll and they always were. My children were well behaved, and they never gave me any trouble. We had a beautiful pool at our apartment. My children loved to swim, and they quickly made friends with other children who lived there. We were settling into this new routine of Florida living which was much easier than living up north. However, I could not attend any Jewish services because of the hours I worked so I didn't have a chance to get to know anyone in the Jewish community.

There were three friends who owned the nightclub. They had been in college and the Navy together. At one point, I thought of quitting the job so I could have a normal life and meet people who were not in the entertainment business. However, my bosses wanted me to stay in the band. They said people liked my singing and it would not be the same without me.

I stayed on for a while longer and started to date one of the owners. We worked the same hours and we got along well. I admired these three men for building this business and they were very good to me. However, I was working in a smoke-filled environment and I was probably not totally recovered from the pleurisy, pneumonia, and mononucleosis. I got sick again and I was working with pneumonia. My doctor called the owners and said, "You are going to have a dead singer on your hands if she doesn't stay home and recuperate." The owners sent me home for a week and paid my salary because they knew I had children and needed the money. I was very touched and really appreciated all they did for us.

Not long after I came back to work, the man who I was dating broke up with me making it uncomfortable to continue to work for them. I was offered another job singing in an upscale restaurant downtown with a smaller band that played easy listening music. It was easier work in many ways because I didn't have to sing over a loud Hammond organ, a trumpet player, saxophone, guitar, bass, and loud drums. This band had a piano player, bass, and drums and we never had any afternoon rehearsals. My voice range returned to normal within weeks of working in this new place. My boss was Jewish, and I was his little Jewish singer. I was treated very well, and I really enjoyed working with this band.

Another New Beginning

About four months later, to my surprise, the man I had dated from the other nightclub walked into the supper club I was working in. This was the first time I had any contact with him since we broke up. He stayed for a long time and listened to our music. When I was done working, he and I went out and talked. He told me that he loved me, and he said he couldn't sleep because he was missing me. He also told me people at the club were asking for me and he wanted me to come back and work for him. Then he proposed to me!

I decided to go back and work for him, but it took me many months to accept his marriage proposal because I had so many fears about getting married again. He sent me out with a realtor to find a house for us to buy. He loved the house I found which was uniquely designed by an architect. We got married by a justice of the peace and my children were happy. The children knew him from the restaurant/club, and they really liked him. My son was missing the father figure and he wanted me to get married. Everything was going well, and we were all happy for about four months.

Little did I know God was about to take me on the biggest adventure of my life!

CHAPTER 3

TWO WEEKS NOTICE

"I know that Messiah *is coming (He who is called the Anointed One). When He comes, He will explain everything to us."*
– Samaritan Woman at the Well to Jesus[6]

One morning, my husband told me a meeting of the nightclub's owners had been arranged, and because I was his spouse, I had to be there. The owner with the controlling interest and his wife who were friends of ours had recently become Christians and no longer wanted to be in the business. When we met, the owner made his intentions clear saying, "I want to sell."

My new husband also made his intentions clear. He looked

straight at me and said, "You and the children have to go. I want a divorce! I am going to buy this nightclub."

I was stunned! I sat there in disbelief! It was totally unthinkable that this man who I loved and married only four months ago, would basically throw us aside as if we had no value so he could buy the business. I was beside myself and my emotions were all over the place. Then he proceeded to tell me he was also going to fire the band, including me. We were on two weeks' notice and he was going to bring in bands from New York. The last thing he said to me at that meeting was he wanted the children and I to leave his house.

It doesn't get any worse than this, I thought. Loss of another husband, loss of my job, and now an eviction notice. At this point, I felt so betrayed by someone I trusted. I went home and called my friend, the wife of the owner who was selling the business.

"I don't understand," I said. "You two become Christians and I get a divorce?"

She told me that was not going to happen, but I told her apparently it was. This time in my life could easily be titled, "Two Weeks' Notice." Everything happened in the next two weeks. The hardest part was telling the children that their new stepfather wanted to own the club and there was no time for a family life. I told them I was sorry, but it looked like we would be going through another divorce.

My husband, however, was acting as if nothing was happening. He wanted intimacy with me and yet he was divorcing me. He told me his dream was to own this nightclub and this was what he was going to do.

It is true that every decision we make in life not only affects us, but all those who depend on us. In my case, it was my children. Every night I had to go to work and sing with the band. I had to smile and act like nothing was happening, but the reality was that my life was falling apart. I felt like I was slipping away. During the day, I kept falling asleep on the couch, something I had never done before. I had always paid my bills, but I never had any savings. I had no money of my own, so I was trying to figure out where I would go and what I would do next.

The first Sunday following that dreadful meeting, I woke up and found a note from our friends, the people who were selling the club. The note said they had taken the children out and I should not worry. They didn't have children of their own and enjoyed being with mine, so I didn't think anything odd about it.

"All you have to do is ask Him to come into your heart and He comes to live in you."

Sometime that afternoon, the children came running through the door. "Mommy, Mommy Jesus loves you," they said. "All you have to do is ask Him to come into your heart and He comes to live in you."

I shook my head and said, “Oh, no, we are Jewish, we don’t believe in Jesus.”

“Why not?” my daughter asked.

“I don’t know why, but when your grandparents call today, do not mention we’re going through another divorce and don’t mention this Jesus.”

“Okay, Mommy,” they said and then ran off to play.

At this point, I was so overwhelmed with my problems, I decided to visit a doctor; one who had come to hear our band many times. I told him I was going through a hard time and I wanted his advice. After telling him what was going on in my life, he said, “This is situational, and you have every right to be depressed.”

He gave me medicine to take, but after a few days I got worse.

I called my younger sister Penny who was in college at the time and told her what was going on and she said I should ask the doctor for Ritalin.

The doctor agreed, but this medicine made me feel wired. I was up day and night. I was a nervous wreck! I decided to throw out all the medications and try to deal with these changes in my life on my own like I always had.

I finally called my parents and told them what we were going through.

My father said, “Three strikes and you are out!”

I knew I was never going to measure up to my father's expectations because

MY LIFE WAS A MESS!

A Huge Piece of the Puzzle: Jesus Is a Jew

Our Christian friends who were selling the night club, invited me to their house to hear a guest speaker, Hal Lindsey, who had just written a book titled, *The Late Great Planet Earth.* He was going to speak to us and show us a slide show of Israel.

Honestly, I went to see the slide show of Israel. There was a house full of people and yet, I felt a lot of peace in that room. We watched the slide show on Israel and, of course, I loved it.

Afterwards, I went to the kitchen to get a drink of water and Mr. Lindsey was there and he started talking to me. After we talked for a while, I told him that I could not accept this Jesus. I said I love my Judaism and the Holy One of Israel, and I didn't want to be a hypocrite.

"Why would you be a hypocrite?" he asked. "Jesus is the greatest Jew who ever lived."

I looked at him in total disbelief for a moment. I had never heard that Jesus was a Jew. Our rabbi never mentioned Jesus' name. I grew up in a predominantly Catholic and Protestant town and many of my friends were not Jewish. They never told me Jesus was a Jew. I am not sure they even knew that truth.

My husband and I talked one night after work. He told me his partner and his wife were trying to get everyone in the nightclub saved.

Then he laughed and said, "You are one they will not get."

Though I didn't fully understand
the importance of what I was saying at the time,
I told him, "We are all doing our own thing,
going our own way, and we all need God.
I am going to find God and turn back to Him."

My soon to be ex-husband shook his head firmly and declared, "Not me."

Although I was not aware of it at the time, there was a big spiritual battle going on over me. I thought Jesus was the God of the Gentiles. I never knew why He was hanging on a cross. Finding out that Jesus was a Jew was a huge piece of the puzzle God was revealing to me in preparation for the next part of my journey.

Searching for God

I was quite excited about making an appointment with the Rabbi of a local Jewish Temple. I just knew the answer for me was turning back to God. There was a ray of hope rising within me and I looked forward to my meeting with the Rabbi. I believed this day would change everything. When the time came, I met with the Rabbi in his office and told him my situation.

"Even my car had rain coming in every time it rained. We call it the 'yuckmobile,'" I told the Rabbi. "In a week, I will be out of work, without a home, and I do not know where my children and I will be going."

I told him I wanted to come back to God, wanted the children to have religious training, and we would be attending Temple services.

To say the least, his response was surprising, "We will need some money for the children to attend religious training."

I could not believe what I was hearing. Did he not comprehend anything I had said? I came and poured out my heart to him and all he could say was he needed money for my children to receive religious training?

He must have seen my reaction because he got very nervous.

"I will try to talk to someone about this," he said.

I walked to his desk, leaned over, looked him in the face and said, "Don't bother, God is not here."

Then I turned and walked out the door. Once I reached the privacy of my car, I sobbed. Now, I was even more depressed and felt that my only hope was gone. I went home and fell asleep on the couch. I was awakened by the front doorbell ringing. I got up and went to the door to find a well-dressed man wearing a suit. He introduced himself as the pastor of the church around the corner and he was inviting me to his church service.

I kind of chuckled as he was talking, so he asked me, "Why are you laughing?"

The truth is I was probably on the verge of a nervous breakdown, but I politely said, "I thought it was funny because I am Jewish."

He immediately apologized and told me to have a nice day.

I turned around and started to walk into the house when I heard a loud voice yelling, "Wait a minute!"

Turning toward the voice, I saw this man in the suit running back up to me.

Then he said something that would change my life forever,
"If you ever go to your own and they turn you away,
you'll know where to come."

A loud gong went off inside my head. At that very moment, I knew I heard from God. I had been crying out to Him for weeks and He was answering me.

No one knew where I had just been, only God! I was very excited and encouraged by this encounter, even though I still did not know what I was supposed to do about my life.

Jer 29:13 says, "And you will seek me, and find me, when you will search for me with all of your heart."[7]

I believe something happened in the spiritual realm that day. This encounter I had was no doubt another piece of the puzzle.

God was moving all along, but I was spiritually blind.

The Next Season of My Life

"Many are the plans in the mind of a man,
but it is the purpose of the Lord that will stand."
– King Solomon[8]

The next week, my husband's partner called. He told my husband to move out of the house and let the children and I stay until the end of the school year. He said he would not sell him the nightclub unless he did, so my husband agreed. I was so thankful for this kindness. This meant we would have a roof over our heads until May when the school year ended. God overruled my husband's "two weeks' notice" ultimatum. This gift from God came through our friends who were now Christians. It also gave me time to find my way into the next season of my life.

God is in control and
His mercies are new every morning![9]

It was hard to work at the club every night. My husband, the band, and all the people I worked with had strangely become my Florida family, and I knew this time with them was coming to an end. I already had too many goodbyes in my young life, and I was not looking forward to another.

Sunday arrived and I woke up to another note from my friends. They had taken the children with them again.

This time when the children came through the door, they said, "We went forward today and gave our hearts to Jesus."

They were each wearing gloves with scriptures of salvation on them and they were so happy. Here we were going through another divorce, changing to another school, and having to endure another move. It did not matter what I felt, I just couldn't take this joy away from them. I just smiled and admired their special gloves.

I immediately called my friends and said, "Now you have done something to my Jewish children. We seriously need to talk!"

They agreed to come over that night and see me. They tried to explain their new-found faith to me, but not much was getting through. I was still depressed and had a lot on my mind. I thanked them for trying to explain things to me and they left me with a book to read. It was about Bible prophecy and the Messiah. It included both the Old Testament and the New Testament prophecies of His coming. I thanked them for their help, and I promised them I would read it.

I Want to Know the Truth

I put the children to bed that night and prayed my own kind of prayer, "Lord, this can't possibly be true that the Messiah is Jesus. The Jewish scholars who study the scriptures would have known. The scribes who copy the scriptures surely would have seen this. I can only believe what I was taught."

Then I said the words that began to set me free, "Nevertheless, I want to know the truth!"

I opened the book and started to read only the Old Testament prophecies. I knew the Jews had written this book. Much later I discovered that the New Testament, except the Gospel of Luke and Acts, was also written by the Jews.

Below are some of the messianic scriptures I read that night.

Messiah would be born in Bethlehem.

Micah 5:2 But thou Bethlehem Ephratah, though thou be little among the thousands of Judah, yet out of thee shall he come forth unto me that is to be ruler in Israel; whose goings forth have been from of old, from everlasting.

Messiah would be born of a virgin.

Isa 7:14 Therefore the Lord himself shall give you a sign; Behold, a virgin shall conceive, and bear a son, and shall call his name Emmanuel (means "God with us").

Messiah's crucifixion scene.

Ps 22:14-18 I am poured out like water, all my bones are out of joint; my heart is like wax; it is melted in the midst of my bowels. My strength is dried up like a potsherd; and my tongue cleaveth to my jaws; and thou has brought me into the jaws of death. For dogs have compassed me; the assembly of the wicked have enclosed me; they pierced my hands and my feet. I may tell all my bones; they look and stare upon me. They part my garments among them and cast lots upon my vesture.

Isa 53:3-6 He is despised and rejected of men; a man of sorrows and acquainted with grief; and we hid as it were our faces from him; he was despised, and we esteemed him not. Surely he hath borne our grief, and carried our sorrows; yet we did esteem him stricken, smitten of God, and afflicted. But he was wounded for our transgressions, he was bruised for our iniquities; the chastisement of our peace was upon him; and with his stripes we are healed. All we like sheep have gone astray; we have turned everyone to his own way; and the Lord hath laid on him the iniquity of us all.

These are just some of the scriptures that I read that night. There are so many more that I won't go into here.

Later I also found out that, the twelve disciples who were called by Jesus were all Jews. They were His students (*talmudim*), who lived with Jesus for three years of His ministry. After His death and resurrection, the Holy spirit came upon them as prophesied in Joel 2:28. They were waiting in Jerusalem in an upper room during the Feast of Weeks, (Shavuot), called Pentecost in the New Testament. They were empowered by the Spirit of God and they became the twelve apostles who brought the Gospel to the known world.

The blood of Jesus was shed to cover the sins of mankind. The Gospel of Messiah is the power of God unto salvation to everyone that believes, to the Jew first, and also to the Gentile (Romans 1:16).

The sacrificial system in the Old Testament was designed by God. God is Holy and cannot look upon sin which is why we need an atonement for our sins.

Without the shedding of blood, there is no remission for sin. God's desire from the beginning was to have the fellowship with man. He has been pursuing us ever since the Garden of Eden. We were made to worship Him and to be in His Presence.

God's desire from the beginning was to have fellowship with man.

Isn't it interesting that there were twelve sons of Jacob, who became the twelve tribes of Israel? Twelve disciples who became the twelve apostles. Then there is the new Jerusalem which descends from Heaven (Revelation 21:12-13) with a wall great and high, and has twelve gates, and at the gates twelve angels, and names written on the gates are the names of the twelve tribes of the children of Israel. The wall of the city has twelve foundations and in them are the names of the twelve apostles of the Lamb.

God is a God of divine order and He has set times and patterns. He is *Adon Olam*, Eternal God!

I cannot remember how many Old Testament prophecies I read that night, but at some point, I stopped reading because I suddenly knew that Jesus was the Messiah. Only He could have fulfilled all these scriptures. I fell on my knees and wept tears of grief.

"How could your chosen people have missed their own Messiah?" I cried.

I knew Jesus (Yeshua),
was The Missing Piece

I called my friends and told them I believed Jesus is the Messiah.

Then I asked them, "What do I do now?"

They came over and prayed the prayer of salvation with me. I asked God to forgive me and to cleanse me of all my sins. I thanked Him for allowing me to see the truth which set me free. There were so many things that I did not understand, but I knew He was God. He was the one my heart was searching for. He was the Holy One of Israel and the lover of my soul. The children and I were born again in 1972.

Ps 139:23-24 Search me, O God, and know my heart: try me, and know my thoughts: and see if there be any wicked way in me, and lead me in the way everlasting.

"Behold, all things are new. Old things are passed away."[10]

The journey I had been on with the losses, the hardships, pain, and suffering were all worth it. I had now found the "pearl of great price"—Jesus! I went to church with our friends and was baptized in the pool at the YMCA. A few years later, I got baptized in the Jordan River in Israel.

I finished my last night singing in the nightclub. Even though it was very emotional for me, I walked off the stage and never turned back. I became a disciple of Christ and never again sang in nightclubs. I now had a new life!

"I tell you, unless one is born of water and spirit,
he cannot enter the kingdom of God.
What is born of the flesh is flesh,
and what is born of the Spirit is spirit.
Do not be surprised that I said to you,
'You all must be born from above.'

For God so loved the world that He gave His one and only Son, that whoever believes in Him shall not perish but have eternal life."

– Jesus to Nicodemus, a Pharisee, Israel's teacher[11]

CHAPTER 4

A NEW LIFE

"Follow Me, and I will make you fishers of men."
-Jesus to His disciples[12]

Because of my encounter with God I now had a new life. The children and I began our journey with God together. The Bible says to walk by faith and not by sight. We really did walk by faith. I can tell you that it was the most exciting time of my life. Is it hard to walk by faith? Yes, it is, but you will never see God moving in your life until you are in that place of total dependence on Him. He is the God of the miraculous. I learned to trust God in ways I would have never known possible. By worldly standards people would say I was poor, but spiritually, I was rich! I finally saw how the hidden hand of God had been leading me every step of the way right to Him! What a glorious rebirth I had.

I became a born-again believer in December of 1972. Remember the "get up and go far away and don't look back" word I heard in the hospital when I cried out to God? That was the call of God. He had a plan and purpose for my life, and He has a plan for your life too. He is no respecter of persons. All we need to do is believe in Him and follow.

"The ruach blows wherever it pleases. You hear its sound, but cannot tell from where it comes or where it goes. God is He, He is Ruach (Spirit) and Ruach is speaking to our ruach (spirit) revealing great mysteries, knowledge, wisdom, understanding and joy."

— Rabbi Sipporah Joseph[13]

Jesus told His disciples to take up their cross and follow Him. I finally found out why He was hanging on the cross. He died and shed His blood to cover our sins. He is our *kippur*, Hebrew word for covering. God is Holy and cannot look upon sin. Hebrews 9:22 says that without the shedding of blood there is no forgiveness of sin.

God Himself sacrificed an animal and He used the skin to cover the nakedness and shame of the sin of Adam and Eve. Then He drove them out of the Garden of Eden, away from His Presence. The skin was a covering (kippurah), the same word as atonement. We are all sinners saved by His grace; we all need a Savior. That Savior was provided by our loving God and His name is Jesus, Yeshua. There is nothing we can do to earn salvation; it is a free gift of God for all who put their trust in Him.

A New Creation- His Plan and Purpose for My Life

After I was saved, all the depression left, and my life was dramatically transformed. I had worked nights for so long and had been living in the darkness as well. Now, I was spiritually awakened and living in the light! I knew a man who used to come to the nightclub with his international business guests and I asked him for a job. I told him I had become a believer in Jesus, Yeshua and I had no desire to sing in nightclubs anymore. He told me he was a Christian, and he could not understand why I had to do this.

I told him that I just got saved and I was on a journey to find out who I was in Christ. He graciously offered me a job. I was now a day person and I loved rising early in the morning and hearing the birds sing. I saw sunrise and sunsets and beauty all around me. God had truly taken me out of the darkness. The weight of the burdens I carried for so long were gone, and I was feeling joy for the first time in a very long time.

At work, I found other believers and we had a bag lunch Bible study. I was now free to be who God wanted me to be; I did not have to try to be what other people said I should be. I wanted His plan and His purpose for my life.

All my choices had led me into a downward spiral of pain, shame, depression, and loss. Now, my new life had purpose and I was full of expectancy and excitement to see what all God had in store for me. The following is one of my favorite scriptures.

For I know the plans that I have for you, declares the Lord. Plans to prosper you and not to harm you, to give you a future and a hope, and when you seek me with all of your heart, you will surely find me and you will be my people and I will be your God. (Jeremiah 29:11,13-14)

After all that God had done for me, it became easier for me to trust Him. Why wouldn't I? He is the Creator and God of the entire universe. In studying His Word, I found out that I was called and chosen by Him; He alone had the right plans and directions for my life.

I finally found the love I had been looking for all my life. I discovered that God's love is unconditional, and He accepts me as I am. This revelation brought me many inner healings, especially with my earthly father.

My only regret
is that it took me so long to find Him!

"The unconditional love of God leads to a life of freedom and transforms each day into a potentially wild adventure."
-Randy Elrod[14]

Making the Right Choices and Wise Decisions

I realize now I had no understanding or wisdom before I got saved. I was blindly going through life making choices and trying to please people, especially my parents. At nineteen, I was too young to be getting married. Any trained counselor would have advised me not to get married. I needed time to grow up and discover who I was. I didn't even know the first man I married.

One thing I have learned through trying to do things on my own for so many years is not to rush into any big decisions. Sometimes, circumstances do not give us a choice, but we can always go to our Heavenly Father for guidance. The Bible says He knows the end from the beginning. He will not steer you in the wrong direction. I heard someone say, "The devil pushes and the Lord leads." How true.

God does not want you to try harder, He wants you to trust Him deeper. Stop trying. Start trusting. This will change everything in your life.

One night, not long after I got saved, I called my sister Sandy who lived in a beautiful home in upstate New York. I wanted to share my new faith with her. She was depressed and said she did not want to live. She had a wealthy boyfriend for years who would not marry her. He was married and it would financially cost him too much to get a divorce. They loved each other, but this was not enough for her. I quickly told her not to do anything and to get on a plane and come see me. I told her that I had the answer.

She said, "Why should I come to see you? You are a mess!"

I agreed with her, but I insisted she come to Florida. She came the next day and stayed with me. I let her talk for a long time and then I told her about the love of Jesus. She cried and said she had never seen me like this. She sensed a peace in me, and she believed what I was telling her was the truth. She let me pray the prayer of salvation with her. Sandy and I had always been close, we were only two and a half years apart. She stayed with me for a few weeks and went back to break off the relationship with her boyfriend. She told him she was packing up and moving to Florida because she had found the love she needed. He asked her who the guy was, and she said His name is Jesus!

He said, "I cannot compete with Him."

She left her beautiful house and wealthy boyfriend to start her new life here in Florida. She was the one who brought me to Florida a year before when I left my old life behind in search of God and a new life. Now, it was her time to experience God in a new and astounding way. I was truly excited for her. My beautiful sister was being transformed by our loving God right before my eyes.

Material possessions, money, houses, jewelry, and cars cannot buy you love, peace, and joy. Only God can fill that empty place in your heart and make you whole. There is healing under His wings and He is a God of restoration.

At the end of the school year, the children and I moved out of my ex-husband's house and into an apartment. I did not see him again for years.

My ex-husband did have a very successful night club. In the beginning, I remember asking God why he was being blessed after what he did to us.

God said, "Do not look back and keep your focus on Me."

Years later, I did write to my ex-husband and told him I had forgiven him, and we were all doing well. Twenty years after our divorce, I heard he had never married, he gave up the nightclub which was his dream, and he was diagnosed with lung cancer. I was very sad to hear this news, but I was glad to hear that he did accept Christ shortly before he died.

It is never too late to accept God's gift of salvation.

It is never too late to accept God's gift of salvation. God is a God of mercy and grace and all are welcome.

I learned how important it is to forgive people who hurt us in life. We need to extend the grace of God to these people. First, God's grace sets us free; grace also releases us to move on. Secondly, God commands us to forgive. Our natural inclination might be to want to get even or to hold on to unforgiveness. The fruit of such a decision not to forgive is continual unrest and turmoil in our own lives. Unforgiveness not only hurts others, it hurts us.

Take Max Lucado's advice in *Grace for the Moment, "I Choose Peace... I will live forgiven. I will forgive so that I may live."*[15]

Trusting God in Times of Fear

Over the summer, we settled into our new apartment and prepared the children to start school in the Fall. My sister Sandy moved into a townhouse a few miles away.

One night, I was meeting a friend and my sister came over to stay with the children. When I got home, she said the children were good and they were sleeping. We visited for a while and then she went home. My children loved their Aunt Sandy and always enjoyed being with her.

We lived in a two-bedroom apartment. My son had his own bedroom and I shared the master bedroom with my eleven-year-old daughter. After my sister left, I got ready for bed and went to sleep. The next thing I knew, I was awakened by a stranger standing over me. He had his hand over my mouth and a sharp knife at my throat! He told me not to scream. My heart was racing wildly, and I was instantly overcome with fear. He started to grope me and climb into my bed, but I motioned for him to take me out of the room and he agreed.

I got on my feet, but I could not move because I was shaking so bad. Fear like I had never known overwhelmed me. Immediately, I silently prayed for God's help! Suddenly, I felt a calmness that came over me and I was able to get him out of the bedroom where my daughter was sleeping. He took me to the couch in the living room and raped me. It was total darkness and I could not see anything. He told me he had been watching me when I was at the swimming pool with my children. He said he knew I was not married and living alone. The sliding glass door was open, and I was very cold. I told him that Jesus loved him and had a plan for his life. He did not have to do these things. He listened to me and then he quickly left. I was so cold and frightened; I could not move for the next few minutes.

When I saw some daylight coming in the window, I got up and locked the sliding glass door. I ran to the bathroom, took a shower, and got dressed before the children got up. I fed them and got them ready for school. I walked them to the bus stop and made sure they got on that bus. Then I got in my car and went to my sister's house and told her what happened. She was shocked and said, "How could God let this happen to you?"

I told her, "No, you are looking at this all wrong. God saved us. He could have hurt my children and ***the truth is we could have all been killed.***"

I thanked God for His protection. Not one time did my children wake up. They were not touched by this pure evil. I went to the police to file a report. Then I went to the office of my apartment complex and told them what happened. I found out this rapist was on the loose and going around raping all the women who were alone in this complex. The management knew about it all along and kept quiet. I was furious and I told them I was moving out immediately. They said I couldn't break the lease, but I told them I would go to the newspapers and tell them everything if they tried to sue me. I felt compelled to go and warn the other women who were living alone in this apartment complex about this dangerous rapist.

Then I rented a truck and some friends helped me move out. We put everything into storage before the children got home. I met the children at the bus stop and told them we were moving in with Aunt Sandy. I refused to tell them about the break-in or the rape. They were much too young to hear any of this.

I am strong when I need to be, but after we were out of that apartment and safe with my sister, I literally fell apart. I was fine all day, keeping busy with moving out, but as soon as it got dark, I was a mess. I went around locking every window and every door twice. Even then, I could not sleep. It took me a long time until I can honestly say I was normal again. I kept praying for God to deliver me from the fear I had experienced that dark night.

I thank God for His everlasting love and healing. Some healings are instantaneous, and some happen over a long period of time. What I have learned from this is to always trust in the Lord. I was such a young believer at this time, only about seven months old, but immediately I knew to call on the Lord. That dark night could have been tragic for all of us. Instead, I saw the Lord save us from the powers of evil and darkness in such a mighty way. Talk about the power of God. Even in this horrible circumstance, He used me to witness to this man. All glory to God!

"Trust in the Lord with all of your heart
and lean not unto your own understanding
and he will lead you in the way you should go."[16]

During the first few years of following the Lord, I had three or four different jobs working in an office. I was unable to keep any job long term, because I could not type. I did all the other office work and I talked to everyone about the Lord. The boss called me in to his office one day and fired me. He told me he felt bad because he knew I had children. I told him, "It's okay. God brought me here for an assignment and my time here is up." My faith had grown, and I knew God had another plan for me.

The Church and the Messianic Movement

I found a non-denominational Bible-believing church. I wanted to learn what the Bible said, and I did not want a religion. I had a relationship with God, and I desired to learn everything about Him. It was such a blessing going to my church. We were there every service and in between I went to Bible studies. Our pastors were great preachers and their sermons helped me to grow in the Lord. Our church became the fastest growing church in the United States. It was an exciting time to see so many lives changed by the power of God, including mine.

Our church started the Jesus Festivals in the Orlando area. People came from all over the United States. The keynote speakers were men like Derek Prince, Bob Mumford, Jamie Buckingham, and so many others. I started reading books by Watchman Nee. Someone had told me his writings were great and that is an understatement. There was such an outpouring of God in the seventies and I was in it. I wanted all of God that I could have because I had such a great need for Him.

Many Jewish people got saved during this specific time and the Messianic movement began to grow everywhere. In every generation, the Lord raises up men and women of God to teach and lead the body of Christ. He gives us pastors, teachers, evangelists, and lay people to help us grow into the full measure of our Lord.

Within three years, most of my immediate family came to Florida and got saved at our church. They got saved, baptized, and went home with Yeshua as their Lord. Even my mother went forward for the altar call and got saved. That same night, she got baptized. She said she didn't recognize what religion this was, but she knew it was Jesus, and she knew she had met God.

After my sister's townhouse lease was up, we moved into a nice house in a good neighborhood she was able to buy. Her teenage daughter Emi lived with us and my sister brought our troubled nephew to Florida. Thank God Brian got saved and lived with us as well. My sister decided to go back to college, and I took care of the house and the children. I started to teach dance lessons at a small private school nearby.

After one year, my sister told me she was selling the house. She said she did not want the responsibilities anymore. When we got home from church the following Sunday my sister said the house sold. She said she was using the money to buy a condominium and her daughter and nephew were moving with her.

God had another adventure waiting for me just around the corner.

CHAPTER 5

ADVENTURE WITH GOD

THE DREAM AND ANGELIC VISITATION

"But if God so clothes the grass in the field which is here today and thrown into the furnace tomorrow—then how much more will He clothe you, O you of little faith? So do not seek what you will eat and what you will drink, and do not keep worrying. For all the nations of the world strive after these things. But your Father knows that you need these things."
- Yeshua in the Book of Luke 12:28-30 (TLV)

Here I go again, another adventure. I owned nothing but my car. I had a dream and I knew it was from the Lord. In this dream there was a specific seven-year time frame. It was about a trip I was going to be taking up the East coast, and it had something to do with spending time with my mother. Then the next thing I saw was my mother's house was all boarded up and she was gone. The dream ended with me returning back to Florida. When I woke up, I researched the biblical significance of the number seven and found that it meant completeness. I stored all of this in my heart as I continued to seek God's guidance for my next step in His plan and purpose for my life.

I had met a man who was a widower with two young children. Their mother died when they were young children, and I felt sorry for them. We became friends and I invited them to church with me. He and his children went forward at the altar call and got saved. A little later they decided to also get baptized. We kept seeing each other and his children started to get very attached to me. I loved the children and I could see their great need for a mother.

After my sister told me she sold the house and was moving, I explained the situation to my friend. He smiled and said he had already been considering asking me to marry him. When I told him about my dream, he told me he had a job offer in upstate New York which is not too far from where my parents lived in Pennsylvania.

He said we could rent a truck and drive there with the children. I knew they desperately needed a mother and all our children were two years apart. They got along very well and to be completely honest, I had nowhere else to go. I accepted his proposal.

I wrote a letter to my father and told him I was getting married again and we were moving up North. "I have been away for a long time and I want to spend quality time with mother. You can drive her to our place, and she can stay for weeks at a time. I don't believe we have much time left with her." I told my Jewish father that the Lord had spoken to me and given me this word of knowledge. We got married, packed up, and headed north to our new destination.

When we got to upstate New York, my new husband found out he did not get the job. However, his parents lived nearby in a very small town and they owned a few houses. They took me to the house they said we could live in. It was very old, and the front porch was falling off. It needed some major repairs. They said they would fix everything and clean it up. They were wonderful and did all the repairs and cleaning, and I had some new carpet installed. We moved in just in time for the children to start school. The local people were amazed at how nice the house turned out.

Summer was over and it was starting to get cold. My husband checked the oil tank and it was empty. We did not have money to get the oil we needed for the winter because my husband just started working a new job. We called the oil company and asked them to come fill the tank. We told them we would pay them as soon as we could. They arrived the next day and told us the tank was already filled. They could not put any oil in it! I believe this was truly a miracle. This confirmed to me that I was where I was supposed to be.

God was showing me once again that
when I seek to do things His way,
He provides what we need when we need it.

Family –The Heart of God

From the very beginning, God's plan was for people to be in families. He told Adam and Eve to multiply and fill the earth. This was the theme again and again throughout the Bible. The family unit was very important then and it is just as important today. I thanked God that we were now a family.

I asked the Lord if I could write music for His glory. This was a desire of my heart for a long time. He answered me, and I have been writing Gospel and Messianic music ever since. I use the music He has given me to worship Him and to bless others. Over the years, I have become a worshiper of the Most High God (El Elyon). I thank God for the gift He has deposited in me. He taught me to play the piano just enough so I can accompany myself when I sing my songs.

Once we were settled in New York, I started having my mother come and visit us. I thank God for the precious time we all had with her. Every day I would read her parts of the Bible. We worshipped the Lord together and had prayer time. She loved being with the children and she came back to see us many times over the course of that year. Our four children seemed to blossom during that school year. My oldest daughter was a cheerleader and my oldest son ran on the track team. He was six-foot-two and discovered this was something he could do well, and he loved it. As a matter of fact, a few years later he and a friend ran one thousand miles in the heat of the summer in Florida.

We were a happy family and the younger children flourished

under my care. I always cooked and they started eating better. I think being a part of a family with routines and schedules was good for them. Their mother died when the youngest child was born, and they were missing the nurturing part of God's love. The truth is they were very good children, so the transition for all of us went well. Our youngest children also had grandparents who lived in the same town; so, they received an abundance of love and encouragement from everybody. My mother-in-law was very talented; she knitted beautiful warm sweaters for all of our children. We were blessed beyond measure; everything we needed God provided.

We were blessed beyond measure; everything we needed God provided.

Looking back on the time we spent there, I can see how much the children learned about life and people. Living in the Orlando, Florida area was all they remembered and almost every house was new and had a swimming pool. The houses had manicured lawns, and everything was in bloom for most of the year.

I remember the day we drove into this town, my children started to cry. They thought the people who lived here were poor because the houses were very old. I said this is normal and most of the Northeast looks like this. I told them these people are not poor, they live a different lifestyle. They canned a lot of their foods and they were wonderful homemakers. Our children made many friends that year and had the best time living in this little town. One morning, I woke up and heard a lot of noise and laughter outside. I quickly got up and looked out the window and saw our four children in their pajamas sliding down the street in the snow. How crazy and yet wonderful and exhilarating was this for our Florida children to experience the joys of their first snow. However, I prayed they wouldn't get sick.

I ministered in a local church where I talked to the children about God. They were surprised when I told them they could pray to God and how special they were to Him. I also told them to expect God to answer their prayers. I found many opportunities to minister Jesus to many people in this small obscure little town. Even though we were only there for one year, it brought joy to all of us. Emmanuel means *God is with us* wherever we go. We are carriers of His love and light. We live in a world filled with fear, turmoil, and uncertainty and Jesus is the answer!

The Angelic Visitation

I sang and spoke at some of the local churches. I found a Bible study group in Ithaca, NY, about forty-five minutes away from where I was living. I joined them so I could keep growing in the Lord. A few months later, I asked them if they would come to our house and I would host the meeting. They said yes and I was very excited. The leader of this group was a wonderful man of God. My mother was visiting us at the time, and she wanted to join us.

Once everyone arrived at the house including a few local people I had invited, we started the meeting with prayer. The teacher was introduced, and he began to teach. My mother interrupted him talking about something that had nothing to do with what he was teaching. He politely listened to her and then suggested we continue with the Bible study.

My mother was a quiet woman who would never interrupt anyone, but on this night she was different. The teacher tried to continue teaching, but again my mother kept talking. I was so embarrassed and didn't know what to do. I asked her to be quiet and listen to the teacher, but she continued talking.

Then I bowed my head and prayed, ***"Lord, send your angels to silence my mother."***

Right at that moment, the kitchen door opened and in came nine or ten angels all dressed in brilliant white. They didn't have wings, but they all were surrounded with an aura of light. They came in single file and floated across the floor. I noticed their feet never touched the ground. The first two immediately floated diagonally across the living room and went directly to my mother who was sitting in a wingback chair. One angel literally sat on her lap and put her arm around my mother. My mother looked up at her and smiled. The second angel stood in place by the same chair. The rest of these angels went to different places in the room and stood silent for the entire time. My mother never uttered another sound for the rest of the night; she was silenced by these angels. Clearly my prayer was answered! By the way, praying specifically is encouraged in the Bible. You have not because you ask not.

To my knowledge, only one other person saw these angels. That woman was frightened, and she immediately grabbed her purse. I was in absolute awe that this was happening because I knew what I had just prayed for. The teacher did not seem to notice a thing and neither did anyone else in the group. These angels said nothing; they just stayed quietly in their places.

When the meeting was over, the angels proceeded to leave in the same way they came. They went out the very same kitchen door in single file. When I asked them who they were, only one spoke. She told me their names were the fruits of the Holy Spirit—Love, joy, peace, patience, gentleness, goodness and faith, meekness, and self-control. After they left, I went outside to see where they were going. They floated down the street in single file and then just disappeared out of my sight. I stood there stunned! What a glorious encounter with God's messengers. How awesome is our God! He even answers small prayers.

After the Bible study, everyone stayed and had refreshments. Not one word was ever mentioned about these visitors. Later, I asked my mother if she saw anything unusual happen during the meeting and she said no. That was amazing, especially since one of the angels sat on her lap the entire time. My mother was very frail and suffering with major heart disease. Obviously, when the angel sat on her lap for an hour and a half, she felt no weight. The beauty of it was my mother was touched by an angel of God. This was a supernatural event in my life that I will never forget. It took my faith to a much higher level. I love to see prayers answered, but this one was over the top! I have learned we must operate in the spirit realm and stop limiting God. He is supernatural and He operates in that realm. When we pray, believe and expect God to answer in His own unique way.

This Was a Supernatural Encounter!

Isaiah 55: 8-9 says, "For my thoughts are not your thoughts, neither are your ways my ways, says the Lord. For as the heavens are higher than the earth, so are my ways higher than your ways, and my thoughts than your thoughts." We have to put our trust in Him. We must surrender and give up control and fully trust Him to lead us. His way is always better. When I tried to take control of my mother's interruptions, it failed to work. When I asked God to intervene, He answered my prayer in the most amazing way.

We must surrender and give up control and fully trust Him to lead us. His way is always better.

Our journey with God should be an exciting one. Unfortunately, some believers never get to enjoy the God of the miraculous because they refuse to give up control of their lives, even to God. The truth is we really do not have the control we think we have. He is God and we are not!

Months passed and once again my mother was with us. My husband lost his job and we decided it was time for us to return to Florida. Orlando was growing in every way and there was plenty of work. My husband went back to Orlando first and soon after we followed. As I was saying goodbye to my mother, she started to cry.

She said, "I am never going to see you again."

I said, "Don't say that, mom, we will come and visit you."

However, like in my dream, she was right! She went to be with the Lord about five months after this visit. Her house was boarded up meaning she was gone, and my father remarried so it became someone else's house. I am so thankful to God for the blessed time He gave us with her that year. When my mother had her heart attack and she was in the hospital, my father would not allow me to come home and see her. All my sisters were home and with her in the hospital. I was the only one not allowed to be with her. My father refused to believe that she was dying and of course a few days later she did.

You see God knows everything and that is why He spoke to me in the dream and told me to go North and spend time with my mother. He gave me time with my mother because He knew my father wouldn't allow me to come home and see her. After my mother died my father felt so bad that he didn't let me come home to see her. He apologized to me many times. I'm glad I listened to the voice of the Lord and moved north that year. The footsteps of the righteous are ordered by God.

After we moved back to Florida and my mother died, my father lent us a small down payment to buy a house. The house we bought needed some work.We cleaned, painted inside and out, and did some renovations. After a lot of hard work, our house turned out beautiful and we lived there for many years. I am a restorer, and love to take broken and unloved things and make them beautiful again. My husband was very handy and together we glorified the house for the Lord. We went back to our Assembly of God church and we all grew in the Lord. We had good times of fellowship with other believers and I was growing in my musical gifting.

Divine Appointments

One day, my husband told me he had called a man who owned the Christian radio station in town. He invited him to come to our home and hear the music the Lord had given me. I sang him one song that was dear to my heart and I could tell he was very moved. He told me this was very anointed, and he thanked us and told us he was going to pray. I felt this was a divine appointment with this man, but I didn't know why.

I failed to hear anything more from him until he and his wife invited me to a "Bless Israel" meeting they were having. For years, I wanted to go to Israel but obviously it was not God's timing. Besides owning the only Christian radio station in the Orlando area, their ministry included taking believers on trips to the Holy Land. They did these trips every year for decades, and they were a real blessing to Israel. The song I sang for him in my house that day was called "Jerusalem." Now I understood why he was so moved when he heard the song. I began to see the spiritual connection.

I went to the meeting that night and I met some wonderful people who were gathered to pray for their upcoming trip to Israel. The leaders showed slides of Israel and spoke about what a spiritual journey it is to go to the Holy land. It became clear to me they wanted me to go on this trip with them. There were three widows there that night and each of these ladies came to me at different times and gave me $100.00. They believed I was going to be on this trip. I was hesitant to take the money, but I refused to get in the way of what the Lord was doing. I told everyone I had to pray and seek the Lord. I knew one day I would be going to Israel, but it had to be God taking me.

I had made mistakes in the past
and knew I had to hear from Him.

Time passed and I basically heard nothing. I was busy with life and raising four children. One morning, I realized the time was up for the deposits for all who were going on the trip. I called the leaders of this tour and told them I didn't think I was going, and I wanted to give the money back to the three widows.

This man, who later became a kind of spiritual father to me, said, "Let's not be hasty. There is still time. Let's wait and see what God will do."

I waited for a few more weeks and called the leaders again. This time they told me that I had a free ticket to Israel, and we would be going shopping for some small music equipment to take with us. I was amazed at the goodness of God. I always knew that when I did go to Israel I would be singing to God's chosen people. I knew beyond a shadow of a doubt that God set up this trip! I had no money, so the good Lord provided everything, including the music equipment. He is Jehovah Jireh, our provider. That is God, He doesn't do anything halfway.

I arranged for the children to be taken care of and I packed my bags and left for Israel. My lifetime dream was coming true. I had no money in my pocket, but as I stood in the boarding line, a woman ran over to me and shoved money in my pocket. I did not recognize her, but she must have done this as unto the Lord. I was going to Israel and our meals were paid for. I lacked nothing. Still, the Lord had this woman bless me. It is so amazing to me that our God is into every detail. I am so filled with gratitude for all He has done.

Baruch ha ba b'shem Adonai.
Blessed is He who comes in the name of the Lord.

The anticipation of what was about to happen was building inside of me as I saw my life's dream coming to pass. The trip over was very long, but I was filled with such expectation. We flew into the Amman Jordan Airport and stayed in a hotel for one night. We had to put our bags outside our rooms at night to be put on the bus early in the morning. The music equipment also was put with our baggage. Frankly, I felt a little uneasy while we were in Jordan. The hotel people were telling us that Jordan was the Holy Land and we should stay there.

However, the next morning after breakfast, we headed to Israel as planned. We had to stop and go through the Allenby Bridge checkpoint. We were greeted by our Israeli guide who was a dear friend of our leaders. They had been using her services for years and loved her. When she saw that we brought music equipment with us, she was upset. The soldiers in charge said we could not bring the equipment into their country. We had to wait for someone higher up to come and inspect this equipment. Our guide told me this delay could take hours. She asked me where I was booked to sing, and I replied nowhere. I was going to sing wherever the Lord led me. I know she was not very happy with me.

First Divine Appointment in the Land

We had a wonderful spiritual group with us that prayed for this obstacle to be removed. About an hour later, an Israeli soldier came to our leader and said that he could not contact his superior officer. He asked if we could set up the equipment and plug it in.

Our leader put his arm around this young man and said, "This lady is a singer and she wrote a song called 'Jerusalem.' Would you like to hear her sing it?"

He said, "Yes."

My first divine appointment in the land. We set up the equipment, turned it on, and I got to sing the song "Jerusalem." There was a large crowd that gathered around me and everything in that place came to a stop. I saw Israeli soldiers weeping as the song pierced their hearts. Some of the words are from the book of Zechariah.

"Jerusalem, Jerusalem, city of old with a story yet untold. Jerusalem your time will come again, you'll see the Glory of the Lord, the Lord your God. Jerusalem, Jerusalem, your destiny's been told by the prophets of old. Jerusalem, your time will come again, you'll see the Glory of the Lord, the Lord your God.

I will return to Jerusalem, and I will dwell in the midst of them, and my Glory shall come and fill thee, I will return again, Jerusalem. Jerusalem will be inhabited as a city without any walls. For I shall be unto her a wall of fire, fire, and my Glory shall come and fill thee, I have chosen you again, O my Jerusalem."

This message in the song is powerful and God's Presence was there with us. I was speechless at how God had orchestrated all this. I had a backpack I carried with the recording of this song. I gave each of the soldiers a copy and everyone else who wanted one. The soldiers said they couldn't keep it because they were on duty and were not allowed to receive gifts. They were holding them close to their heart and didn't want to give them back. I told them we would find a way to get it to them when they were off duty.

What I failed to realize at the time this was happening is that these soldiers were not sure if the music equipment had a bomb in it. Good Lord, I never thought of that. Why would I? I am American and do not live in their dangerous world.

Psalm 121:4 says, "He that keeps Israel neither slumbers nor sleeps."

"Dear God," I prayed, "Watch over them."

Our Israeli guide and I became good friends after this. I taught the people on our tour bus some Israeli songs and we all had great times together. When you are in the land, the Holy Spirit manifests itself in different places. Some people breakdown at the Sea of Galilee. Others have their encounters with the Lord at the Garden Tomb. We took communion in the Garden Tomb and prayed with people from many other nations. Everywhere we went there was such a beautiful Presence of God with us.

For me, the place of His Presence was the wall. Think of it, I had waited a lifetime to be here in this very place. I was surrounded by so many Israelis praying and seeking their God at the wall. What a blessing and yet, I was grieved in my spirit to see this picture of His chosen people praying in this Holy place. It was a powerful moment and yet, it left me with a deep sadness in my heart because they do not know their own Messiah Yeshua, (Jesus). Have mercy, O Lord on Your people, Israel. Remove the blindness from their eyes so they may see You in all of your glory.

Our Israeli guide asked me to sing several times at different places we toured. She even invited me to her house with our precious leaders. I did share my faith with her as time went on. We saw each other for many years after this trip and we remained dear friends.

The next day, as we were on our way to Metula, Lebanon, we started seeing a large convoy of Israeli soldiers and tanks on the road. We asked what was going on and they told us it was just military training. When we got to the hotel for the banquet, we saw the entire hotel guarded by soldiers with Uzi rifles. A little excitement for our tour which was not boring by any means. We had dinner with some high-level Israeli officers seated at the head table.

After dinner, I had the honor of singing for these soldiers. I sang "Jerusalem." Once again, the anointing was on every word I sang to them. I watched these strong brave men of Israel weep as the words penetrated their hearts. This was another divine appointment of God. Even the staff from the kitchen came out to hear me sing and they, too, were touched. I saw how God was using this music He had given me to reach His people's hearts. He was speaking to them through the music. I believe Israel invaded Lebanon the day after that banquet.

All too soon, our wonderful tour of the Holy Land came to a close and it was time to go home. Before we left Israel, we had to go through the same Allenby check point where we first started. A few Israeli soldiers came on our bus and requested that I sing for them again. I asked them what song they wanted to hear, and they replied "Jerusalem." I played the soundtrack of the song and sang it once again. This was a very emotional moment for me. To think that they even remembered me, or the song after two weeks had gone by was a surprise. Both entering the country of Israel and leaving Israel, God had arranged for these divine appointments. In humility I can only say thank you (todah) in Hebrew to our Mighty God. I am truly honored that you would use me.

A Prophetic Word

I was tired when I arrived home, but so glad to see my wonderful family.

A few weeks later, I got a phone call from a woman I didn't know.

She said, "The Lord told her to call me and tell me that my music was going to be on a shelf for a very long time. Your music is prophetic, it's for a specific time and the Lord doesn't want you to get discouraged."

I was not aware of what prophetic was. Forty years later, I can tell you she was right. One thing I have learned is God's timing is perfect and His will, will be accomplished. I have been on this journey for a long time and I sense as the times get much worse for Israel, many prophetic words and music will be released. I pray it will give them hope and turn their hearts back to God, the Holy One of Israel. They need to put their trust in their Messiah. His Hebrew name is *Yeshua* (Jesus).

The Holy One of Israel will be coming back again to one place on this earth and that place is Jerusalem. This is the only piece of real estate that God has chosen to place His name. This is where He died for the sins of the world, and this is where He will return to save His people, set up His kingdom where He will rule and reign FOREVER. God has two witnesses on the earth today, Israel and the church. The Lord wants His church to be one body with Christ as the Head. He wants the wall of partition between the Jew and the Gentile to be broken down. He calls this the One New Man (Ephesians 2:18).

We believers in the church are to pray for the Jewish people who don't know their Messiah. Today, there are many Messianic congregations in the United States and all over the world. There are small Messianic congregations throughout Israel. We have to pray for this move of God in Israel and elsewhere to be unhindered. Prayer is essential for any move of God, but especially in Israel. The spiritual battle that goes on there is powerful because they are on the front lines. The enemy doesn't want the Lord to return to Jerusalem and set up His kingdom. He knows that his time is short. **Remember this is a spiritual battle.**

(Rev 19) When God Almighty returns, He will be riding on a white horse with a two-edged sword in His mouth. On His thigh is written the King of kings and the Lord of lords. As His feet touch the earth, it splits in two.[17] Such is the power of our God, He is the maker of Heaven and earth. We need to line up with what God is doing and make sure we are praying according to His will.

All believers should be able to discern the times we are now living in. We are living in exciting times that we never thought we would see. We have a God-given mandate to prepare ourselves for the prophetic times we are in.

We must know the Word of God,
and be empowered by Him.

When *Yeshua* the Messiah left and ascended to Heaven, He sent us the Holy Spirit. We need to be sure we are born again and filled with the Holy Spirit. Without the Holy Spirit, we are powerless. There is a spiritual battle going on between the forces of darkness and light (God).

The end of the Bible tells us that God wins. I pray the body of Messiah will get on our faces in an attitude of humility and repentance and pray. God desires that all would be saved and come to the knowledge of His Son. The Gospel must go to all the world which includes His chosen people Israel.

I pray the body of Messiah Jesus will become one body, unified like never before. Let us come together to seek the Lord and pray. Remember, we were born for such a time as this.

God desires that all would be saved, and none would perish.

CHAPTER 6

TESTIMONY AND MUSIC

They overcame him by the blood of the Lamb
and by the word of their testimony,
and they did not love their lives even in the face of death.
(Revelation 12:11 TLV)

I was invited to be the guest speaker at one of the Women's Aglow meetings. They wanted me to share my testimony and sing some of the music God gave me. The next thing I knew, I was booked at many Aglow chapters all over the state of Florida, parts of Georgia, and even in Ohio. The first time I shared my testimony, it was emotionally hard on me because it felt like I was re-living it. As time went on, I began to see how my story was helping so many women who had their own struggles to overcome. My testimony gave them encouragement and hope!

God uses everything in our lives for His purposes, the good, bad, and the ugly. The time we shared together was intimate and anointed. Tears were shed in the sad parts, but they also rejoiced when they heard how God moved in my life in awesome and miraculous ways. To God be all the glory. I do not know how many times I heard this over the years, but at the end of these meetings, the women told me I should write a book. The women were right, but the timing was off. Looking back on it now, I can see why it was not time. There were many more chapters and years ahead of me that I had to live before the book could be written.

Since my gift was writing music, I never thought that I would be the one writing the book. God has a way of getting us to do things we know we are not capable of in our own strength. He stretches us in ways beyond whatever we think we can do in the natural and He uses us in spite of ourselves and our weaknesses. God uses ordinary people and makes them into extraordinary people so they can do great things for the kingdom of God.

I would like to say that the Women's Aglow International ministry was and is one of the most powerful ministries for women all over the world. I believe the vision for this was right from the throne room of God. Through this ministry, women from all different denominations and backgrounds and women who were not even saved, came together to seek God. It was a beautiful safe place for women to share with each other and minister God's unconditional love to those who were hurting. Many unsaved women came to these meetings and found their Savior, Jesus.

The Harvest Is Plenty, the Workers Are Few

For the next seven years, I went to two nursing homes after a call came to our church asking someone from the choir to come sing and minister. I was the only one who said yes. It was great training for me. I took my music equipment once a month and went to encourage them. The first time I went, I asked one of the nurses who will preach?

She said, "You are all we have. Just keep your eyes on Jesus."

Some of the residents were not in their right minds and I had to ignore their antics. The people who I was there for were loving it. I got to pray the prayer of salvation with so many of them. The harvest was plentiful, and these wonderful people were soon going to meet their maker. My pastor said no one was going to fight me for this platform. He was right, but I was the one being blessed. I looked at it as a unique opportunity to help change their lives for eternity! God desires for all His people to reach out to those who need to know Him. All we need to do is keep our eyes and ears open for our own unique opportunities to use our gifts and talents to serve Him.

Obedience Brings the Blessing

One day, I got a call from a woman who invited me to come and sing at the Jewish Community Center. They were having a Chanukah celebration. I told her that I would love to, but I also told her that I was Messianic, and I wrote my own music. She insisted

I come, and I gladly accepted, but at the same time a part of me thought this is crazy.

The night before I was going, a friend of ours came to our house and said, “Tomorrow when you sing ‘Jerusalem’ to these people, they are going to give you a standing ovation.”

I had to hold back my laughter thinking they are more likely going to run me out of town. Nevertheless, the next day I went with the hope of being a blessing to the Jewish community. They welcomed me and sat me at a table near the back of the room. The program started and they served latkes, which are like a potato pancake. One of their men took the microphone and he talked about the Chanukah story. After about ten minutes of this, they started shouting at him to shut up and sit down. Instead of sitting down, he continued speaking, and then they started throwing their latkes at him. Looking back on this scene, it was somewhat humorous.

I was a little nervous watching this knowing that I was next on the program. I wondered if they would be throwing their latkes at me. Right at that moment, the women who invited me got up and introduced me and told them I was going to sing for them. I walked to the front of the room and sang a Jewish song they knew so we could do a sing along. Then I sang one of my own songs which had a Hebraic sound. At this point, I started to talk to them and told them that I was raised Jewish, but I had also met my Messiah, Jesus (Yeshua).

To my surprise, they were very quiet. They were listening to everything I said. I told them God loved them and He wanted to meet with them.

I said, "You are His beloved chosen people. Go home and get your Bibles out and start to read God's Word. He will speak to you through His Word."

Then I told them I was going to sing a very special song I wrote called "Jerusalem." I also told them I was a lover of Israel and had been to Israel many times. I sang my song "Jerusalem" to a music track and you could have heard a pin drop. They were so quiet and listening to every word of that song.

When I was done, I turned around to turn off my music equipment and I heard all this noise coming from their chairs moving. I turned around, and to my amazement, they were all standing up and giving me a standing ovation. I was amazed. Although they did not know it, ***the standing ovation was for God***. He took a chaotic situation and calmed it down enough so they could hear and feel His presence. After it was over, I gave each of them a copy of the song "Jerusalem" and they graciously thanked me. A group of them ran after me and followed me out of the building and into the parking lot.

They asked, "Who are you? This was so spiritual and uplifting."

Then another one asked, "Are you one of those born-again believers?

I said, "Yes, I am."

One of my Jewish friend's mother was there that day. She came home and told her daughter that they were all talking about me for weeks after that Chanukah celebration. They loved the song "Jerusalem" and could not believe I freely gave it to them. God is good! (*Tov in Hebrew*).

All glory to Him who sits on the throne forever and ever.

I am so thankful God entrusted me to minister to His precious chosen people. It had an impact on them and me. All glory to Him who sits on the throne forever and ever.

What did I learn from this? I learned that when God sends you on an assignment, He will minister through you. His anointing changes the atmosphere and we have nothing to fear. Remember that obedience brings the blessing. In the natural, I wanted to run out of there, but God does not operate in the natural realm.

Everything about God Is Supernatural!

"If you tell God no because He won't explain the reason He wants you to do something, you are hindering His blessing. But when you say yes to Him, all of heaven opens to pour out His goodness and reward your obedience. What matters more than material blessings are the things He is teaching us in our spirit." - Charles Stanley

More "Bless Israel" Trips

Meanwhile, each spring I went on the Bless Israel tours to Israel. I was so honored to have the leaders Al and Elaine Chubb, as my friends. They encouraged me so many times when I desperately needed it. They were like my spiritual parents. They blessed so many people over the years with the Christian radio station they ran and all their other good works. I am certain that God loves people like them who unselfishly give all for the kingdom of God. I know for a fact that they gave it all. They poured into me and countless others over the years.

Any time there was something going on for Israel, Al would call me and ask me to sing "Jerusalem." Pastor Ken Garrison, who was a great teacher, would bring the message. Pastor Garrison had a very big heart for Israel. The Lord used him and his Fellowship Church, to be a channel of blessing to the Jewish people in the land for decades. God allowed me to learn and grow from all these great men and women of God and I am forever grateful.

Radio station WAJL, We Acclaim Jesus Lord, was founded by Al and Elaine Chubb. "We consider that we are a ministry first, a business second," Chubb said. "Our goal is to honor God in all things, to pursue excellence while improving the quality of Christian broadcasting. BLESS ISRAEL TOURS, LLC was born out of a love for Israel, the God of Israel and the Word of God."[18]

I went on five trips to Israel with the Bless Israel Ministry. Each trip was unique and different. During a trip on El AL airlines from New York to Tel Aviv, I had a beautiful experience on the flight.

It was nighttime and I was in the back of the plane sleeping. Early in the morning, I woke up surrounded by many Israeli men in their prayer shawls. They were saying their morning Hebrew prayers and I was in their midst feeling the beautiful presence of God. This was a unique experience and I was deeply moved. If I was seated anywhere else on that plane, I would have missed this blessing. This year's tour was wonderful because we got to see other places we had not seen on our previous trips. You cannot see everything in Israel in one trip.

A God Encounter

Our tour group went to the wall to pray on the Sabbath. I was standing alone watching the Jewish people pray. Suddenly, I was crying and then the crying turned into uncontrollable sobbing. It was heart-wrenching! Some of our people on the tour came running over to me and asked me what was wrong. I was not able to answer them because I was crying so hard. Our leaders told the group to leave me alone. They said the Spirit of God was all over me and they were right. When we left the area and got back on our bus, the crying subsided until I looked back at Jerusalem and the sobbing started all over again.

When we got back to our hotel room, I was so drained I was unable to go to dinner. I had to be left alone for a while and hear from God. I've never experienced this type of encounter before where I couldn't speak. I believe I was grieving in my spirit for the Jewish people. This stayed with me for several days and had a profound effect on me for the remainder of the trip.

After I got home from Israel, the Lord told me the spirit of intercession had come upon me at the wall. I was grieving deeply for the lost sheep of the house of Israel. I sat down at the piano one morning and the Lord gave me a beautiful song called "The Wall." The lyrics and music to this song are powerful.

I have had this type of encounter happen to me only three times in my entire life. Let me be clear, this is not something you can make happen. This is initiated only by God. The Spirit of God completely takes you over and makes intercession for us with groanings which cannot be uttered.

Trips to the Holy Land are life changing. I tell people to be sure you are going with someone who is spiritual and go expecting to meet God. Stay away from the large tours. They are rushed, noisy, and too busy to linger to experience God in any of the holy places. Be sure to prepare yourself by spending time in the Word daily before the trip. Have a childlike faith, put your hand in His, and let Him show you things in the spirit you have never seen. I often pray, "Open my eyes Lord, so I can see what You want me to see and give me understanding."

Finally, pray Psalm 122:6, "Pray for the peace of Jerusalem, they shall prosper that love you."

Pray for the Peace of Jerusalem

(Psalm 122)

A Song of Ascents. Of David. I rejoiced when they said to me,
"Let us go to the House of Adonai."
Our feet are standing in your gates, Jerusalem— Jerusalem,
built as a city joined together.

There the tribes go up, the tribes of Adonai
—as a testimony to Israel—
to praise the Name of Adonai.
For their thrones for judgment are set up, the thrones of the
house of David. Pray for the peace of Jerusalem—
"May those who love you be at peace! May there be shalom
within your walls—quietness within your palaces."
For the sake of my brothers and friends,
I now say: "Shalom be within you." For the sake of the House of
Adonai our God I will seek your good

Our Need for God Will Bring Us Closer to Knowing Him Intimately.

Time passes quickly and somehow the days and months turn into years. Our children were growing up and my oldest daughter Susan left for college in North Carolina. Unfortunately, my husband began to lose interest in the things of God. He started making excuses and didn't want to go to church anymore. He was doing great at work, but something in him had really changed. Here I was on fire for God and my husband seems to be going in the opposite direction.

I prayed for him and we eventually sat down and talked about what was going on. All he could say was he wanted to go out and have fun. His idea of fun was going out to nightclubs, dancing, and drinking. He wanted me to go back to the night clubs with him. I told him that was not an option and I would never go back. From that time on, we started to come apart. Meanwhile, I tried to keep the house and children as normal as possible. They were not young anymore and they knew something was wrong between us. Every night, he would find something to get upset about and then use it as an excuse to go out. This behavior went on for months and became a nightly routine.

Our Choices Will Determine Our Destiny

That spring, I made my last trip to Israel with the Bless Israel Ministry. We went to the new Christian Embassy in Jerusalem. When all the embassies moved out of Jerusalem, Christians decided they would stand with Israel and they birthed this ministry. We met wonderful leaders who were the founders. One of them was Jon Willem Van der Hoeven. He spoke to us at one of the evening events. He was a powerful man of God! This man was prophetic and his knowledge and insight in the Bible were undeniable. He was the keeper of the Garden Tomb for years. He is a gift to the body of Christ.

I shared my troubled marriage with some of the leaders on the tour. The last night we gathered, Jon Willem anointed my head with a vial of oil and prayed a powerful prayer over me. His last words I remember were, "Lord, line him up with your will or remove him."

The next day, we flew home to our beloved USA. When I arrived home, my husband was standing at the top of the stairs telling me he had divorced me while I was gone. He told me he wanted his freedom. I was emotionally devastated. I was very worried about our youngest children and how would they be able to cope with a divorce. They had already lost one mother, and now they were going to be losing another mother and siblings. Months later, I remembered the dream I had about the seven-year trip I was going on. We got married in 1974 and moved North for one year. Now, it was 1981. Our marriage lasted exactly seven years.

My daughter was away in college at this time, so my son and I moved into an apartment. I signed over our beautiful home to my ex-husband hoping he would stay there with the children. I thought this would help give them some stability. The agreement said he had to pay me back the money my father lent us to buy the house. I got that check and immediately sent it to my father. He gave me the car we had which was almost paid for. I was extremely tired and emotionally drained from all of this.

After all our hard work to be a loving family and follow God, buy and restore our house, my husband's selfish decision to be single again brought us heartache and destruction. Satan comes to steal, kill, and destroy. Jesus comes to give us abundant life. It's all about our choices, and eventually our choices will determine our destiny. Choose this day whom you will serve. There is no turning back for me; for me to live is Christ.

After all this happened, I heard that my ex-husband immediately sold the house at a high price and moved. At this point, all I could do was pray for them. Occasionally, I was able to briefly see our youngest daughter. Her father would drive her to see me on his motorcycle. I only saw her briefly and it was usually small talk because he was always right there with us. I never got to see her alone. She was growing up and her brother told me she quit high school and went to work. She must have been extremely depressed because just two years later, she took her own life. What a tragedy; she was so young. When my ex-husband called to tell me the sad news, I was up all night crying. The only thing that gave me any peace at all, was the fact that I knew she was saved.

God knew that she would die young. I am so glad that I met them, and they got saved and baptized. I am also thankful that I married their father and got to be their mother for those seven years. Her brother who was older, moved out of state a year after the divorce and made his own life. He kept in touch with me for many years and he was happy and doing well. The last time I saw my ex-husband, he told me that I was the best thing that ever happened to him and his children.There are consequences for our actions and one wrong decision affects the entire family. We are responsible for how we live our lives.

I was guilty of getting divorced from my first husband. What I have learned about divorce since then is that God hates divorce. It tears up families, and family is the heart of God. I knew when they came out with the no-fault divorce law that this would cause even greater damage to families. It's too easy to get a divorce.

The breakdown of the family has been the strategy of the enemy for decades.

I know we cannot go back and undo the past, but we can learn from our mistakes and make better choices. I have had many inner healings over the years that I have been with God. He is our healer, deliverer, our comforter, and our restorer, and I am living proof of this truth. His arms are open wide, and He is our loving Father. He is the God of the second, third and fourth chance. If we repent and turn back to Him, He will always welcome us home. Many of the songs I've written have been birthed out of some of the most painful times in my life. I have shared them with others going through their own struggles. We are called to minister to hurting people wherever they are. We are the body of Christ and the love of God is what people need. We all need Jesus!

There are no perfect Christians.
We are all sinners saved by God's limitless grace.

CHAPTER 7

HEALINGS AND RESTORATION

He was pierced because of our transgressions,
crushed because of our iniquities.
The chastisement for our shalom was upon Him,
and by His stripes we are healed.
-The Prophet in Isaiah 53:5 (TLV)

My son and I were living in a lovely quiet apartment. He graduated from high school and planned to go to the University of Florida in the Fall. My daughter completed her first year of college in North Carolina and then transferred to the University of Florida. You can save so much money by going to a state college because out of state tuition is double the cost. This coming Fall, they would both be at the same school. Some of my friends asked me how I could send my kids to college when I didn't have any money.

I said, "How can I not send them? They are both bright and they are college material. This is the United States of America and my children are going to go to college."

God guided my decisions and both of my children had the opportunity to get a college education.

While I was living with my son that year, I started to have abdominal pain. I went to see my OB-GYN doctor. He examined me and said I had to have a hysterectomy. I asked him if he believed in God and he said yes, he was a Methodist.

I told him, "God is going to heal me because I do not have any medical insurance."

He hesitantly said, "I hope so," but I knew he did not believe it.

I went home in a lot of pain and soon the women in our Bible study heard about my situation. They not only prayed for me, but they brought food to us as well. Then they held garage sales in my garage over several months to make money to pay our bills. It was so humiliating for me to be in this position, but I truly was thankful for everything they did. My son was a part of this, and I know he was trying to encourage me.

He would say, "Isn't this great? It's so exciting to see what God is going to do next."

This went on for about two or three months. The pain was so bad, I was crawling on the floor because I could not stand upright.

One night, I was in bed reading my Bible and I heard the Lord say, "Go to the piano."

The piano was in the front living room far away from my bedroom. Even though I was in pain I got out of bed and crawled down the hallway to the living room. I managed to pull myself up, sat down at the piano, and the Lord gave me a song. The words and music poured out of me and I wrote it down as fast as I could. The title is, ***"By His Stripes I Am Healed." I got up from the piano and I was totally healed! Hallelujah!*** The pain was suddenly gone and never came back. To this very day, I have never had that hysterectomy. All glory to the One who sits upon the throne!

My mother and two of my sisters had hysterectomies when they were young. Afterwards, they were put on massive amounts of hormones. At that time, that was the medical treatment recommended. They all died in their late fifties and early sixties of massive heart attacks. Looking back on this time, I honestly believe that God spared me from having that operation. I have outlived them by twenty-seven years. I have a younger sister who is also living, and she has never had a hysterectomy either. I am convinced that not having that operation saved my life.

It is so important to listen to the Spirit of God when a situation in your life comes up. I cannot say this enough, obedience brings the blessing. We are talking about life and death situations and it is imperative that we develop the ability to hear the voice of God.

We must bypass our mindset and thoughts and get quiet enough so we can hear His voice and direction.

We need to learn to be led by the Spirit of God. He is an all-knowing and all-wise God. He is the God of the miraculous, we must simply believe.

Once again, we see the faithfulness of God.

Then Yeshua came down with them and stood on a level place.
A large crowd of His disciples and a multitude of people, from all Judea, Jerusalem, and the coastal region of Tyre and Sidon, had come to hear Him and to be healed of their diseases.
Even those disturbed by defiling spirits were being healed.
Everyone in the crowd was trying to touch Him, because power flowed from Him and He was healing them all.
– Luke 6:17-19 (TLV)

In May of 1982, my son Darren graduated from high school. He left to go to the University of Florida at the end of the summer. He was a delight to me, and I knew I would really miss him. It is hard to see your children grow up and leave home. I loved them dearly and they were gifts given to me by God. No matter how hard our lives were, we were the three musketeers. We helped each other and were very close. I taught my children to be givers and they always were.

During this same time in my life, I met a wonderful woman of God and we became dear friends. Ruthann was a very loving person. She had a daughter who sang, played guitar, and wrote music. Ruthann asked me if I would listen to her sing and tell them what I thought. She came to see me and sang one of her songs. I immediately saw the great potential in her. I called her parents and told them I had no doubt that she would become a star. I told them she would either make it with her singing or her writing talent. I was right, she is very successful as a writer in the music business and I still love her singing voice.

After my son left for college, Ruthann and her husband Len had me move in with them and I became a part of their wonderful family. Their children and mine, who were all close in age, became very good friends. I believe God put me with this family to see a healthy marriage. They were Christians and they were like a breath of fresh air for me. I just needed to be a part of a fun-loving and Godly family. I will never forget their kindness and I am so very thankful God allowed me to be a part of their lives.

One day, Ruthann told me she and her family were moving to South Florida because her husband got a good job offer. They were going to sell their house and wanted me to live there and take care of it until it sold. This was another blessing from God. All I had to pay for was the electric bill. I was happy for them, but I also knew I would miss them. I was able to visit them a few times after they moved. Ruthann contacted some Aglow chapters in South Florida, and I was invited to be their guest speaker.

The women's Aglow is an international Christian ministry. I was also invited to a luncheon with a pastor from a large church in Miami. We met with about six or seven other people who were in ministries and the pastor interviewed each of them as we ate lunch. I was the last one he talked to but honestly, I felt like the least one of these ministries. I was surprised when he turned to me and said, "This Sunday, I want you to come and minister to my church."

When I arrived at the church, the pastor asked me to also share with a women's group before the service. I met with these women and shared parts of my testimony and we prayed together. Then in the main service the pastor asked me to share my testimony with the congregation. When I was done, the pastor asked me to continue to minister as the Lord led. The only thing that God put on my heart was a call of repentance. I asked the congregation if anyone had anything against any Jewish people whom they knew whether they had been hurt by someone who was Jewish or worked with someone Jewish who had offended them. At this point, I saw so many getting out of their seats and coming down to the altar for me to pray for them.

This was totally a move of God I did not expect. There was a true spirit of repentance there and I saw many of them weeping as they asked the Lord to forgive them. I told them it is time to forgive and let go of the past so they could move into the destiny and calling God had for them. We prayed together and I am sure it was precious in God's sight. They were set free that day and now I understood why the pastor had chosen me to minister in his church. We ended with a beautiful prayer for the salvation of all Israel. I had never ministered in such a big church before that day. It was a very big stretch for me, but I am honored that I was given the opportunity to be used for God's glory.

One thing I have learned from this experience is that God knows exactly what He is doing even when we don't. It is all about trusting Him.

Getting back to my friends, their house in Orlando didn't sell and it turned out to be a blessing because the job they moved for didn't end up working out long term. Thank God they had their home to come back to. They told me to stay with them until I knew where I was going. I ministered in several churches and ladies' groups throughout central Florida. I also cleaned houses and condos for a while.

Another unique experience I had was when a man from a church I knew asked me if I would come and sing some of my music before he did the teaching. I said yes. I only had enough gas in my car to get to this church across town and I had no money. I went to the church and I sang some of my songs I had written. The man who invited me thanked me for coming and said the church gave him an offering and he didn't need it. He told me the Lord told him to give it to me. I thanked him and I was grateful for God's goodness once again.

Another man stopped me before I left and introduced himself to me as the church choir director. He told me he was going to do a big musical cantata and after hearing me sing that night, he wanted me to be one of the soloists. I told him to send me the music and I would gladly be a part of it. He sent me the music to the song I would be singing, and I loved it. We also discussed the slides and pictures I had of Israel. He told me they were going to use three large screens with beautiful pictures as the background for the music. I gave him all the slides and pictures I had, and he used them. He told me a famous conductor from Nashville was coming including a team of technical people.

I went to the first rehearsal and sang the song assigned to me. The choir said I sounded just like the recording and they were happy. Three weeks later, the choir director called me and told me his soloist was very sick and could not do the cantata. The performance was only ten days away. He asked me to take her place and be the soloist for the entire performance. That meant learning many songs in ten days and to be honest, the music was harder than the song I was doing. I told him that I didn't want to do it. He said he had no one else who could learn all this music and he was sure I could do it. It seems to me that the Lord continues to put me in situations that are far beyond what I can do. I do not mind being stretched because this is how we grow, but this was such a big event and I was way out of my comfort zone. I reluctantly said yes, and I had to learn a lot of music before our next rehearsal. Some of the music was a duet with a male vocalist who was a guest coming from out of town. We would only have one rehearsal together and then the next night was the performance.

It seems to me that the Lord continues to put me in situations that are far beyond what I can do.

The next problem was I didn't own a gown. A sweet sister in the Lord took me shopping and bought me the gown and shoes. God supplies all our needs according to His riches in glory. The team came from Nashville and the famous conductor turned out to be David Clydesdale. He was the young brilliant arranger and conductor for Sandy Patti. We met lovely people who were a part of this team and they were excited we were doing this cantata. The music in this cantata was very beautiful and I was blessed to be a part of it. The giant screens with the pictures were a lovely addition to the music, and spiritually, it took us to another level. I heard the Lord speak to me that night and He told me that one day, I would be doing something audio visual.

All of this came from me saying yes to a teacher in a church who wanted me to come sing some of my music. I said *yes* even though I only had enough gas to get there. When God opens a door for you to go through, you never know where it will lead. He has many blessings waiting for us if we will go in faith and be obedient. Faith is a verb and we must step out of our comfort zone and act on it. Do not let fear or past failures stop you from reaching out for all that God has for you in this new season. We have been called and chosen and we all have a destiny to fulfill. Listen to the prompting of the Holy Spirit. The Holy Spirit will lead us and guide us to the exact place we need to be for God's purposes. One word of caution, in order for us to be led by the spirit, we cannot have our own agenda. We have to die daily and be hidden in Christ and from that position, the spirit of God will lead us and reveal to us His plan and purpose.

Healings and Restoration

I started to have some problems with my heart. I went to a Cardiology group and they told me I was having irregular heartbeats, bad palpitations, and I had to go on medicine. My children were going to the University of Florida in Gainesville at the time. I called my daughter and told her I thought I should go home to Pennsylvania for a while.

She said, "No, you should come up to Gainesville and we can live together."

She was in nursing school and said, "We have Shands Medical Center right here."

After I prayed, I decided this was God's answer for me. I went to college with my kids, who does that? My daughter and I rented a townhouse; it was the sweetest time for us. I got the best care with a very good heart group in town. I applied at the University for a secretarial job and had to take a typing test. I flunked it two times. In the meantime, I met some lovely Christians who were praying for me and on the third try, I passed. I felt like God moved me to Gainesville for a time of healing and restoration. The doctors did put me on medicine to regulate my heartbeats, but I was exhausted all the time. I believe all of the stress I had endured in my life had taken a toll on me. Gainesville was God's place of rest and healing for me.

I started work at the University and I really loved it. The people I worked with were all wonderful. The Lord knows what we need even when we don't. I was now married to Jesus and loving it. He is the best husband anyone could ever have.

"Do not fear, for you will not be put to shame,
And do not feel humiliated or ashamed, for you will not
be disgraced. For you will forget the shame of your youth,
And you will no longer remember the disgrace of your widow-
hood. For your husband is your Maker,
The Lord of hosts is His name;
And your Redeemer is the Holy One of Israel,
Who is called the God of the whole earth. For the Lord has
called you, Like a wife who has been abandoned, grieved in
spirit, And like a wife [married] in her youth when
she is [later] rejected and scorned,"
Says your God. – The Prophet Isaiah in Chapter 54:4-6 (AMP)

As time passed, the heart palpitations improved, and I was able to be on less medicine. We found a Baptist church to attend and we loved the pastor. We also met a couple at the church who found out we were Messianic. We became very close with this family and I thanked God for their love and friendship.

One day when our new friends came to our townhouse, they said, "Look, even her walls cry out Jerusalem."

I also had pictures of rabbis studying the Holy scriptures. I thought rabbis had the closest relationship to God. I remember praying in Israel many times asking God, where is my rabbi? These people became our dearest friends. I sang for them for some of their gatherings and they had a deep understanding of God's people, Israel. I was being healed and restored in every possible way: in my body and my emotions. I had a good job with medical benefits, and I had paid vacation times. I lived in Gainesville for four years. It was a sweet refuge for me and for the first time in a long time, I was stress free.

One night at our prayer group meeting, they prayed for a husband for me. I reacted badly. I told them I was married to Jesus and did not need a husband. They said I was in ministry and I needed a covering. I went home and the Lord showed me my reaction came from the fact that I didn't trust men. After all I had been through, who would? I asked the Lord to heal me and I apologized to my prayer group. I know my life is not my own, Lord I pray your will be done.

We laughed so hard we cried. The three of us shared whatever we had.

The years we lived in Gainesville will always be so special to me. When my son Darren was able to eat dinner with us, we had a great time. My daughter was in nursing school and she would tell us the funniest stories. We laughed so hard we cried. The three of us shared whatever we had. My son was into the football games and one year they won the SEC championship. Go Gators!

Another God Encounter

One day, I was out on the porch praying and I started sobbing uncontrollably for my ex-husband, the children's father, who I did not even like. I was down on my knees praying for him and I could not stop crying. I failed to understand what that was about, but I knew it was God. This was the second time in my life that the Spirit of God had taken me over with groanings and sobbing.

About an hour after this episode was over, I got a call from my ex-husband, the children's father, telling me his mother called him after years of not talking to him. She asked him to come to see her right away. She lived in New York and he lived in Washington, DC. He jumped in his car and drove to see her, but when he got there, he found her dead. He was sobbing on the phone with me and my heart went out to him. Now I knew why I was praying for him.

He called me back a few weeks later and asked if we could see each other if he came to Florida. He wanted to know what happened to us. I thought it was a little late after eighteen years had gone by, but I quickly discerned that the Lord wanted this meeting to happen so He could bring healings to all of us.

He came to Gainesville and spent time with us. He and I went out and talked everything through for hours. I reminded him of how badly he had treated me, and he said he was sorry. He said he was young and foolish and owned up to not giving me child support. He confessed that at the time he wanted to get back at me. I told him that he hurt his children and we all struggled. My children were a little upset to see us together again and they asked me what was happening. I told them not to worry. I knew that God was doing some healings between us that were long overdue. I didn't know the extent of it, but I knew God was in it. I believe our long talks cleared up many issues we had with each other and I was thankful for that.

He called me a few weeks later and invited me to Washington, DC to see him perform. I went and it was a very nice weekend. Watching him perform was like going back in time. He was still very charming and talented, but that was all. I said goodbye to him and flew back to Florida. A few weeks later, he called me again and asked me if I would marry him. I was totally taken by surprise and didn't know what to say. I thanked him for the offer, and I told him I was happy we had made peace and put the past behind us. I told him that it would never work because I was all about God, and he was not. He was still an atheist.

I have learned that only God can make healings like this happen. These healings that happened between us were very important for our entire family. You see, God is working in our lives even when we are not aware of it. In my humble opinion, the most important healing that took place that weekend was between he and I. Remember, this was a man who did not pay his court ordered child support for years. He also took my inheritance and severed my relationship with my Aunt who I loved. He lied to her and she took me out of her will while she was dying of cancer and left it to him. He tried to hide that, but in time it all came out. None of these things were trivial by any stretch of the imagination.

To forgive is a choice and I knew that God wanted this to happen. My ex-husband received my forgiveness because of God's grace. This healing that happened between us allowed my ex-husband to walk our daughter down the aisle on her wedding day which was only five years later. Then twelve years after that, my ex-husband died a terrible death of cancer. He left my daughter and a stepbrother an inheritance. Weeks before he died, he called me, and he was crying. He wanted to tell me how sorry he was for everything. I told him he needed Jesus, my forgiveness he already had. Just as unforgiveness adversely affects us and generations to come in a negative way, forgiveness on the other hand brings peace and wholeness and countless blessings into our lives. Forgiveness is always the best choice!

Do not grieve the Ruach ha-Kodesh of God,
by whom you were sealed for the day of redemption.
Get rid of all bitterness and rage and anger and
quarreling and slander, along with all malice.
Instead, be kind to one another, compassionate,
forgiving each other just as God in Messiah
also forgave you.
– The Apostle Paul in his letter to the Ephesians 4:30-32 (TLV)

There are future things in our lives that only God knows. We are called to be peacemakers. You do not want to block your blessings because you refuse to forgive. My ex-husband remarried a wonderful woman and I was happy for them. I prayed for him until the day he died.

Though I made many mistakes along the way, my children and I ran the race God had set before us.

Therefore, since we have such a great cloud of witnesses surrounding us, let us also get rid of every weight and entangling sin. Let us run with endurance the race set before us, focusing on Yeshua, the initiator and perfecter of faith. For the joy set before Him, He endured the cross, disregarding its shame; and He has taken His seat at the right hand of the throne of God. Consider Him who has endured such hostility by sinners against Himself, so that you may not grow weary in your souls and lose heart. (Hebrews 12:1-3 TLV)

I encourage you not to grow weary or lose heart. Yeshua is the initiator and perfecter of your faith.

The Prodigal Son

My typing skills improved greatly while working at the university because that was a big part of my job. Having a steady job really helped me to have a sense of self-worth. I could now pay my bills. I never had a credit card which turned out to be a blessing. I lived on my paycheck and had no debt. I got paid vacations and loved being a small part of something big and wonderful. My bosses had doctorate degrees in agriculture. They went to different places all over Africa and taught the people how to grow food and different crops. To me, they were like missionaries. They treated me very well and I respected them all. My time in Gainesville was very uplifting.

My son had an older car at school which he could not drive because he could not afford it. Instead, he had a bike which worked out well since everyone on campus was riding bikes. However, I began to see big bruises on his legs, and I asked my daughter what they were from.

She laughed and said, "Mom, he is falling off his bicycle because he is getting drunk."

He was going to the fraternity houses and he ended up joining one. He was not going to church with us and I knew he was backslidden. He had a girlfriend who was beautiful, but I did not know much about her. I kept him in prayer as any mother would. I now knew this was another one of God's big reasons for bringing here me to Gainesville. Prayer is essential for any breakthrough in your life.

One day my son came to me and told me he was having trouble in his relationship with his girlfriend. He wanted to break up with her and he wanted my advice. I told him he needed to be honest with her.

My son was in a very hard major and his girlfriend was struggling with school. College can be hard on young people. They broke up and as time passed, they were able to be friends.

A Miracle Happens

Not long after this, a miracle happened! My son called and wanted to go to church with us. When he arrived at church, he was in sports clothes looking very disheveled and he smelled of alcohol. We sat on the front row of this Baptist church. My son leaned over and asked me if I had any mints. I told him I did not, but even if I did it wouldn't help. I know he must have been so embarrassed. When the service was over, the pastors came to meet my son. I thank God for men of God who discerned this young son of mine was lost. They were so loving and accepting to him that day. We must always accept people who come to church as they are. God does, shouldn't we?

After church, he went home, and I did not say anything. I let God do the work. Later that afternoon, I got a call from my son who told me that **he made the biggest decision of his life, he was giving his life back to God.** He told me that he never wanted to be poor. His goal had been to make a million dollars and he did not care who he had to step on to get there.

Then he said, "I've been drinking and not living for God, but now that's changed. I have to read the Bible and know God's Word for myself. From now on no more drinking."

He also told me he had to tell his fraternity brothers about his faith in Jesus. I told him I was proud of him and that he had made the right decision.

He said, "Mom, you know me. I am all or nothing."

He was a track runner and yes, he was an all or nothing type of guy.

Does God Answer Prayers? Yes, He Does!

The Bible says, "The prayers of the righteous availeth much" (James 5:16 KJV). So, do not give up, mothers and fathers, pray and then pray again for your children. Do not let the enemy take your children. Try to keep the lines of communication open with them no matter how old they are. Be an encourager. Today, more than ever, there is so much out there to take them down. The forces of darkness are everywhere. Most of all, they need your love and acceptance.

Double Graduation Day

In May of 1986, both of my children graduated on the same day from the University of Florida. If I had the money, I would have rented one of those airplanes to fly over the stadium with a sign on it saying, "THANK YOU, JESUS!" What a victorious day for them and me. They had done work-study programs, taken out student loans, won scholarships, and every summer they worked to earn tuition money. I was so proud of them and God was with them through it all.

My daughter graduated from the college of nursing with high honors and became a pediatric nurse. My son graduated with an accounting degree and a few years later became a CPA, Certified Public Accountant. He followed in his grandfather's footsteps. I am so proud of their achievements. Like any parent, all I wanted was a better life for them. The best gift of all was my son's decision to repent and live for God. Their father and some of my family members came to their graduation and we all celebrated together.

My daughter got her first choice, a job in the pediatric department of Shands Medical Center in Gainesville. My son returned to the Orlando area and got a job there. I stayed in Gainesville with my daughter for one more year.

I was still very active with my prayer group. We went wherever prayer was needed. I called us the God Squad! We had some very sick children we were praying for. We were also ministering to the parents going through this with their children. Some of them, I'm sorry to say, didn't make it and that was very hard on the families. The stress on them is almost unbearable. They needed God and His unfailing love.

My daughter took care of many young children who had terminal illnesses such as cancer, cystic fibrosis, and aids. I remember the first time I saw her at work as a nurse. She was taking care of a very young child and I had to leave the room to cry. She was such a good nurse and the children and parents loved her. She received letters from many of these parents thanking her for her good care and compassion. What a calling! Thank God for good nurses!

CHAPTER 8

LED BY THE LORD

My presence will go with you, and I will give you rest,"
Adonai answered Moses. But then Moses said to Adonai,
"If Your presence does not go with me, don't let
us go up from here!"[19]

Prophetic Words from the Lord

One night, our prayer group had visitors. It was a pastor and his wife I had met once before. We enjoyed each other's company and after our meeting was done, they had a word for me.

They said, "The Lord told us you will be doing a big production."

I did not want to receive this word and told them, “I don’t know anything about productions.”

They said, “You went to Juilliard for dance.”

I said, “That was a million years ago. I write music and sing and that’s all.”

Then I got a call from a Women’s Aglow in South Florida to be their guest speaker. I accepted the invitation. This was the first ministry I had done since moving to Gainesville four years ago. It was so wonderful to be sharing with these beautiful women. When the program was over and I was packing up to leave, a few of the women asked if they could pray for me.

I said, “Of course, I would love it.”

The woman who was their worship leader said she had a word from the Lord for me.

She said, “You are going to meet your husband. He will be everything you are not, and you will be everything he needs. Together in the hands of God you will be used for His glory. This is going to happen soon; it’s not a longtime off.”

I thanked them, said goodbye and drove back to Gainesville. The word that was given to me got filed away. I was so happy these past seven years married to Jesus, I honestly did not think about it.

About four months later, I felt God was telling me to go back to Orlando. My prayer group in Gainesville did not agree, but

I knew I heard from God, so I said goodbye to my wonderful friends and my daughter.

My Orlando friends whom I had lived with before said I could stay with them until I got a job. I had wonderful references from my bosses at the University. I could type very well now, and I was trained and ready for an office job.

Birth of Messianic Congregation

I received a call from a man from my church who said, "I would like to hire you to be my secretary. We are starting a Messianic congregation here and I want you to be a part of this. I cannot pay very much, but I need you."

I thanked him for the offer, but I turned him down. He was not married, and I really did not care for his personality. Also, the pay was awful, and I didn't want to be poor again.

The next day, I went on an interview for a job and they liked me, but I did not get the job. Then I went on a second interview and that went well. They offered me the job and I accepted. I went to work on the first day and they told me they were sorry, but they changed their minds and were going to use someone else.

The third job interview I went on went well, but I never heard from them either. This is not what I expected. In my spirit, I discerned something was wrong. I had a good cry, prayed, and asked God to show me where I went wrong. I repented of anything I had done and told God I will do whatever You want me to do. Not five minutes later, the phone rang, and it was the man from church, the job I didn't want.

He said, "Lana, I know you said you wouldn't work for me and I know the pay isn't good, but I need a secretary who has a Jewish background."

I said, "Yes."

He continued talking, then suddenly realized I had said something, and he asked, "Did you say yes?"

I answered, "Yes, I will take the job."

He was so surprised and happy. The other reason I did not want to work for him is I was afraid the Lord would have me marry him.

He then told me he was taking his girlfriend to a conference that weekend. Great news!

I had just learned another lesson. I thought because I was trained, I could go and get any job I wanted, and I did not need God for this. That independent thinking will always bring trouble.

We must be led by the Lord because every decision is important. You see, ***it's all about our destiny!*** We must be in God's will and He alone directs our path.

I am so glad I was obedient and took that job. Now I pray, "Lord, when everything is going wrong, help us to stop and seek You. You know the beginning and the end, and I don't."

I have learned that God's Word is our road map for living our lives. The Holy Spirit leads us and guides us into all truth.

The Ruach Reveals Truth

When the Spirit of truth comes, He will guide you into all the truth. He will not speak on His own; but whatever He hears, He will tell you. And He will declare to you the things that are to come.[20]

Looking back, I can see that once again, God was leading me to where He wanted me. The job interviews I went on were done in my flesh. I didn't bother to ask God where He wanted me. Being in the right place at the right time is crucial. It is dangerous to make decisions based on our own limited knowledge or feelings. ***We must learn to hear the voice of God for ourselves***. That is why we have to learn God's Word. He is the living word. I have made so many costly mistakes by not going to God.

One night, a prophet told me that I was a man-pleaser and God wasn't happy with me. That word brought me to tears of repentance! From that night on, I became a God-pleaser. I have failed a few times since then, but I have grown in this area over the years. God is my first love and priority.

In 1988, we started the first-ever Messianic services in our church. This was an exciting time for many Jewish people were coming to the Lord. I was the leader's secretary and I was on the worship team. After I started work, I moved into a small apartment. Everything was going well, and the congregation was growing.

My boss came out of his office one morning and said to me, "Lana, I believe God is going to bring you a husband in my synagogue."

I said, "I see. You think God can only bring me a husband through your congregation?"

He said, "No, but I believe this is how it will happen."

About two weeks later, I was running late for the service. I parked my car and our worship leader parked next to me. He introduced me to a man he had brought with him to the service. I quickly ran ahead and didn't pay much attention to his guest. We had our usual sweet service and at the end, our leader told us to hold hands and pray for each other. The worship leader's friend was standing right next to me. When we closed our eyes and started praying, I felt like an electric current going up and down my arm.

I heard the Lord say, "This is your husband."

Oh, my, goodness! I thought.

After the service, we had an *Oneg Shabbat*. This was a time of fellowship with some cake, cookies, and drinks. I was responsible for that, and I was busy serving people.

This visitor who came with our worship leader walked over to me and asked, "Do you ever sing "Amazing Grace?"

I said, "No, we don't sing "Amazing Grace" here. It is a beautiful song, but we are a Messianic congregation and we are an outreach for the Jewish people. We sing Hebraic and Messianic songs."

I remembered hearing that this visitor was Jewish.

So, I asked him, "Where do you go to church?"

He said, "I go to a Baptist church."

I asked him if he had ever been to Israel and he said no. I told him I had been there many times.

He walked away for a while, then came back and said, "I perceive that you are a holy woman of God and I would like to get to know you."

Then he and the worship leader said goodbye and left.

That night when I went home, I called my best friend and told her I had met my husband. I told her everything that had transpired and the word I received from God. She was surprised because she knew I had not dated anyone in seven years.

She asked, "Who is he?"

I told her, "I don't know."

I have a confession to make. I went home that night and I talked to God and said, "I don't think this man is a rabbi. I don't even know what kind of a Jew he is."

Then I reminded God, "If I am to be married, I will have to be equally yoked. That's what Your Word says! Lastly, I have a call on my life and what kind of a call does he have?"

Finally, when I came to my senses, I was thankful that God did not strike me dead. After all, who am I to question my maker, the God of the entire Universe? The next day, I went to work, and all was well. The following Friday, I was getting everything set up for the service and two Spanish women who attended our congregation called me over.

They said, "Lana, the Lord showed us that new visitor who came last week is going to be your husband."

"Good Lord," I thought. *"Who else knows this?"*

I just smiled at them and walked away.

I thought to myself, *"I don't even know who this man is. I don't even know his name. This is craziness!"*

The next day was Saturday and I got a phone call from the man I met at our congregation. He told me he was in town and wanted to know if we could meet somewhere and get a cup of coffee. He wanted to see me.

I said yes, but I was nervous. I had only been back in Orlando for a few months and this was happening so fast. I had not dated in seven years and I was not comfortable being with a man.

We met at a Denny's restaurant up the street from me and talked for hours. He was a gentle, soft-spoken man from what I could see. He told me he lived in the Daytona area and he was a medical doctor. He said he had been married and had children who were grown, and he was divorced. He was raised Jewish and was from the Bronx, New York. He was interested in the Messianic movement and that is why he came to our congregation. I loved the flow of communication we had between us. I discerned he was earnestly seeking a deeper relationship with God. We talked for a long time and then said goodbye. After this, I continued to watch God move.

Show Me the Rabbi

The following week, I was selling tickets for our Passover Seder. He bought only one ticket. I asked him if he would like to sit with my family at our table. He said it would be an honor. I arranged my first date with him with spiritual ulterior motives. At the last minute, my boss told me I had to go to another table and babysit someone's children. I said no, I wanted to be with my family. He asked me who else I was sitting with and I told him Dr. Barry.

He said, "Take Dr. Barry with you to this other table" and I did.

Passover is a major Spring Feast of the Lord celebrated by Jewish people all over the world. Christians who are not familiar with this Feast know it as the last supper. Jesus and His disciples were actually celebrating the Feast of Passover. During this Passover meal, the Lord Jesus instituted Holy Communion. Jesus shared this with His disciples for the very first time. He told them to eat the unleavened bread (*matzoh*) and drink from the cup of wine in remembrance of Him. He told them to do this often in remembrance of Him.

This Feast is about God's deliverance for the children of Israel from four hundred years of bondage and slavery in Egypt to freedom. An unblemished lamb was slain, and its blood was applied to the doorposts of their houses. When the angel of death saw the blood on their doorposts, it would "pass over" them. Thus, the name Passover. The Jewish people were delivered out of Egypt by the hand of God and led into the wilderness to worship Him. He miraculously parted the waters of the sea and led them through on dry ground. They were poor slaves for four hundred years, but when God delivered them, they left with the wealth of Egypt. Now fast forward to the time of Christ. Jesus in obedience to His father, offered himself as the unblemished sacrificial Lamb of God. His blood was shed to cover our sins. Leviticus 17:10-11 says without the shedding of blood there is no remission of sin. We who were in bondage to sin, are now set free by the blood of the sacrificial lamb of God. His name is Jesus, Yeshua.

He miraculously parted the waters of the sea and led them through on dry ground.

I could hardly wait for the Passover service to begin. I asked the Lord to show me the rabbi I had prayed for. The Seder service began, and we started to read from the Haggadah (order of Service). I looked at Barry sitting across from me and ***I saw the rabbi!*** Yes, the Hebrew and the Holy scriptures flowed out of his mouth and that is what I needed to see. This sealed it for me! God's word is true, and I knew He was the rabbi I had prayed for.

After some painful hard lessons, I have learned to let God have His way and I will not put my hand to it. I knew this was a God thing and He would bring it to pass in His way and in His timing. I never told Barry what the Lord told me. That word was hidden deep within my heart.

Barry continued to come to see me on the weekends. Our favorite meeting place was Denny's restaurant where we sat and talked for hours. He was always a gentleman and I felt very comfortable with him. He was intelligent and a very good communicator which I loved. One night, we went on a date to see a Christian concert. Many times, we went to the beach and took some sandwiches and drinks in a cooler. We did simple things and our times together were wonderful and wholesome. He attended our Messianic services weekly and everyone liked Barry.

When my two children met him, they said "What is there not to like?"

One Friday night, our leader announced that Barry was going to Israel to a Messianic conference on Shavuot. That is the Feast of Pentecost, the outpouring of the Holy Spirit and the birth of the church.

I looked at Barry and he asked, "Do you want to go with me?"

I said, “No, this is your trip. You do not need any distractions. I am overjoyed for you.”

I must admit I was a bit surprised at how fast this was happening. I absolutely knew this trip was going to be life-changing for him.

We spent most Saturdays together and I loved spending time with him. He came to my apartment one Saturday and he told me that he enjoyed being with me, but he was going to be a medical missionary. He did not want me to get hurt. He had dozens of applications out and he was sure he was going to be leaving.

I asked him if he wanted to stop seeing me.

He said, “No, I love being with you.”

I never told him what God told me about us. Some things are better left in the hands of God.

Barry’s Spiritual Trip to Israel

A few weeks later, Barry left for Israel and he told me when he came off the plane, he got down and kissed the ground. This trip turned him inside out and upside down. It was the trip of his lifetime. These believers from the United states, and the Jewish believers in the land were called to come together at this specific time and place for God’s purposes.

It was 1988, the fortieth anniversary of the State of Israel. It was also the Feast of Shavuot, (Pentecost). This was the first Messianic Jewish conference in Jerusalem in 1900 years. Think of how amazing this is. Many young Israelis believed in Yeshua, but because of the fear of persecution, they were hiding their faith. When they heard about this conference, some of them came from all over Israel and participated in this event. They were ministered to by many powerful Messianic leaders from the United States and Israel who encouraged them to go deeper with their faith. After this conference, scores of small congregations were birthed in Israel. God was truly calling for more believers in the land to be courageous and not be afraid. The presence of the Holy Spirit was strong and there were many prophetic words given. One of the Messianic leaders told Barry he was going to carry a torch for his people, Israel. God was going to give him the platform and the means, and he would have healing hands. The man who gave Barry this prophetic word didn't know that Barry was a medical doctor. This trip was life changing in many ways for Barry. This is when he got baptized in the Holy Spirit. He was now a spirit-filled believer. God is Tov, the Hebrew word for good.

Barry called me from Israel and said, "I am not going anywhere. You and I have the same calling and God is putting us together for His purposes."

He was crying so hard it was difficult to hear him. This was confirmation for me that God indeed was putting us together. I had known it for some time, but more importantly, Barry had to know it as well. How wonderful that God had spoken to both of us separately. That is the way it should be.

Remember, at this same time he had dozens of applications out to be a medical missionary. To this day, many years later, he has never heard from one!

I remembered the word from the Lord given to me by the worship leader from the Aglow meeting nine months earlier. "You are going to meet your husband. He will be everything you are not, and you will be everything he needs. Together, in the hands of God you will be used for His glory. This is going to happen soon, it's not a long time off."

God's Plan for Our Lives Will Unfold

God's plan for our lives will unfold in His way and in His timing. Barry's gift is teaching, and he has mercy gifts. My gifts are in the arts and I love to sit at His feet and worship Him. I am a worshipper of El Elyon, the Most High God. Together in His hands, we are to be used for His glory. However, before God uses any of us, there is a time of preparation and sanctification. He prepares us for the ministry He has called us to.

We were about to enter this time of preparation.

Even youths grow tired and weary,
and young men stumble and fall,
but they who wait for Adonai
will renew their strength.
They will soar up with wings as eagles.
They will run, and not grow weary.
They will walk, and not be faint.
-The Prophet Isaiah[21]

CHAPTER 9

THE PROPOSAL

The Rest of the Story

Two months after Barry's return from Israel, he called and told me he made reservations for us at a fancy French restaurant. He told me to get dressed up because this was going to be a very special occasion. He showed up at my apartment with a huge bouquet of beautiful flowers. As we were driving in the car, he seemed to be nervous. I suspected this was the night he was going to ask me to marry him. When we got to the restaurant, they seated us in a secluded alcove that was very picturesque. He looked so handsome in his white dinner jacket and bow tie and I was excited. He ordered us a glass of wine that we sipped on.

Barry said, "Do you want the good news first or the bad news?"

I said, "I want the good news."

He said, "I brought you here tonight because I was going to

propose to you."

Then he took a box out of his jacket pocket and showed me the ring.

Then he said, "I don't think I can ask you to marry me because of what happened today."

He proceeded to tell me that earlier that day the FBI came and arrested him on disability fraud charges. They drove him from Daytona to the federal courthouse in Orlando where they officially charged him with twenty-eight counts of Social Security disability fraud. Each of these charges carried a maximum penalty of five years in prison. That total came to **one hundred and forty years.** Yes, 140 years! After this happened, he went back to Daytona, bought me flowers, got dressed, and came to Orlando for our special date.

I knew about the accident he had many years ago. He was driving an old jeep pick-up truck in Virginia and another car came too far over to his side and he was forced off the road. He rolled over in his jeep several times down a small mountainside. He ended up landing upside down in a shallow stream and he had to be pulled out by people who rescued him through a window. Of course, he was badly injured in several places and he could not work.

He had private disability insurance which he had paid for and was entitled to. He also applied for Social Security disability. He filled out the applications and went to their doctors for testing. Because he was a doctor, he knew how to answer their questions and he may have exaggerated his condition. Who knows, he was in pain and he was a complete mess at that time. He was injured in many places. He had severe headaches, neck and back pain, and some short-term memory loss. He was approved for the disability which he received for seven years. He did not work during this time.

The prosecutor, on the other hand, didn't believe he was injured at all and he was determined to make a big case against him and his wife. Every check he received in the mail was considered a federal charge. After seven years, the case against him and his ex-wife was ready. The very day the FBI charged him ended up being our engagement day!

God's Plan and Strategy

Lean on, trust in, and be confident in the Lord with all your heart and mind and do not rely on your own insight or understanding. He who deals wisely and heeds [God's] word and counsel shall find good, and whoever leans on, trusts in, and is confident in the Lord— happy, blessed, and fortunate is he.
– From the Proverbs of Solomon[22]

When we finished talking, I reminded Barry that we already knew the Lord was putting us together and I accepted the ring. ***One thing I knew, our relationship was ordained by God***. I told him that God would have us go through this together. Two are better than one. We still had our engagement dinner and I encouraged Barry to trust in God. I told him God is on our side and we will be victorious! I truly believed this. We got engaged in July of 1988.

In November of this same year, I had my first and only car accident. I was driving on a local street and a car went right through a stop sign and hit my car. I couldn't stop and the accident was inevitable. I had severe whiplash and bruises, suffered with headaches day and night, and had neck and back pain. The doctors put me on pain medicines and muscle relaxers which helped, but I couldn't do anything. This went on for many months.

Barry was living in the Daytona area and was trying to help me. He was going back and forth and paying my bills because I was unemployed. He found a law firm to represent him and he had many meetings with them. I could not be in these meetings with his lawyers because I was not his wife. After watching this, I sought the Lord and asked Him what we should do. I wanted His plan and strategy.

He said, "Get married!"

Never doubt God's mighty power to work in you and accomplish all this. He will achieve infinitely more than your greatest request, your most unbelievable dream and exceed your wildest imagination! He will outdo them all, for his miraculous power constantly energizes you.[23]

Under the Chuppah (*The Canopy of God)*

In January of 1989, I told Barry the Lord said we were to get married. He was reluctant because he thought I could be left with a husband in prison for a long time. I said, "That is not going to happen." He agreed and in four weeks, we had our beautiful Messianic wedding at our congregation in the church. We were married under a chuppah and we had both a rabbi and a pastor marry us. Our congregation and our families were invited. To my surprise my father said he wanted to come to the wedding. My lovely daughter Susan was my maid of honor and my Jewish father walked me down the aisle to my favorite song, "Great is Thy Faithfulness." My son Darren told me he thought the Messianic wedding was absolutely beautiful. He welcomed the guests and said some very kind words.

After the ceremony was over, we had a reception at the church. I was a very happy bride and Barry was the most handsome groom. It was more than I could have asked for because it was spiritual and beautiful. God is the best matchmaker and His ways are good (*tov*).

We planned our two-day honeymoon at a lovely hotel in the Orlando area. However, when we arrived, we found the room was dark, dingy, and expensive. I told the gentleman at the desk this was our honeymoon and we were not happy with our room.

He said, "I will do something special for you."

He gave us the **penthouse suite** for only two hundred dollars more. This penthouse rents out for a thousand dollars a night. God is good. He sent us trays of food, wine, and champagne. He said someone had ruined his honeymoon and he wanted ours to be great. It was more than I could have ever asked for. The suite had giant windows all around with spectacular views. I love how God moves for His children.

Best of all I had my rabbi, the most Christ-like man I know. All of my family agreed that Barry was the rabbi I had prayed for. Everyone loved him. During the first few months of our marriage, God brought us many prophets, both men and women, who spoke into our lives. The amazing thing is that every word they spoke over us came to pass. I saw God move so powerfully through those hard times. You know, when our need for Him is the greatest, He shows up and does miraculous things.

You know, when our need for Him is the greatest, He shows up and does miraculous things.

Barry and I were and still are a good match. His giftings are wonderful and mine are, too, but they are different. We got married in February and his trial was set for June. I asked the Lord early on in my walk for wisdom and discernment. I wanted to be able to understand what was happening in the realm of the spirit. Now that I was his wife, I attended every lawyer's meeting. I needed to hear where they were going with the case. The Lord was so gracious giving me explicit words of knowledge and insights into Barry's case.

Our lawyer was a young brilliant Jewish man. He loved Barry and I knew that God was using him. He and his wife went to Australia for a vacation and he took Barry's case with him so he could study it. That is dedication!

This case was complex and had many facets to it. I told our lawyer early on that God was on our side and He was going to remove the prosecutor who was going after Barry with a vengeance. The prosecutor was planning to make a spectacle of him.

I also told the lawyer, "You will see the Lord remove him from this case. I know because I have received a word of knowledge from God!"

Of course, he did not believe me, but I knew in time he would see the miraculous God we follow.

It is so wonderful that even in the midst of our troubles, the Lord uses us to be His witness.

The prosecutor continued to prepare for the upcoming trial and so did we. I had prayer warriors fasting and praying and they were going to be in that courtroom with us.

A few weeks before the trial, we had a meeting with our lawyer down at the courthouse. Barry and I were sitting in a hallway waiting and we heard a lot of laughter going on in one of the rooms.

When our lawyer came to meet us, we asked him, "What is

going on in that room."

He said, "They are having a going away party for the prosecutor who is leaving."

I looked at Barry and then said to our lawyer, "The prosecutor is leaving? Do you remember what I told you several times?"

He said, "Yes, he is leaving, but he will be back for your trial date."

I smiled and knew deep in my heart that ***God was moving him out!***

These are the moments in our walk with God we never forget. God is into every detail of our lives. He has it all under control and we only need to believe.

I'll say it again. *He is God and we are not.* We must move out of the way and let God work on our behalf. In our case, I knew God was going to do something supernatural and wonderful for us. That does not mean we won't pay for our wrongdoing. It does mean He will watch over us and be with us every step of the way. The Lord chastens those who He loves, He is a good Father.

It is very important that our belief in God is strong before trouble comes our way. Things are going to happen in life even to those who have done nothing wrong. That's why we must be strong in the Word and have times of intimacy with God. He will move Heaven and earth to help those who belong to Him.

The Spirit of the Lord goes to and fro over the earth looking for one whose heart is towards Him. Revelation 3:15-16 says, "I know thy works, thou art neither cold nor hot: I wish thou were cold or hot. So then because thou art lukewarm, and neither cold nor hot, I will spew thee out of my mouth." Let us pray, "Lord, help us and prepare us for this journey with You. Teach us Your ways, O God. Help us to walk in paths of righteousness all of the days of our lives and show forth Your glory."

Psalm 46:10 says, "Be still and know that I am God." It is all about Him. We only get one chance at fulfilling our destiny. May we gladly surrender to His Lordship in our lives knowing He will work all things out for our good.

And we know [with great confidence] that God
[who is deeply concerned about us]
causes all things to work together [as a plan]
for good for those who love God,
to those who are called according to His plan and purpose.
- Apostle Paul's letter to the Romans[24]

The Battle Belongs to the Lord

As Barry and I were preparing for this trial date, some decisions had to be made. We were told there were new government guidelines for sentencing. You could either accept these guidelines before your trial or reject them.

Barry's mindset was, "I am not guilty, and I am not going to accept these guidelines."

I did not have a peace about this. Barry and I talked. I told him I would not put the fate of my life into a worldly judge's hands. This would allow the judge the freedom to sentence him up to one hundred and forty years. I would gladly accept these guidelines knowing the worst-case scenario would only be fourteen months. I told him we are in this together and I will not allow you to make this decision on your own.

I told him to get alone with God and pray and ask Him what to do. He came to me the next day and said the Lord told him to accept the guidelines.

Barry wisely chose to accept the new guidelines and I thanked God we were now in unity. These new guidelines also had to do with the amounts of money received over the seven years. If the amounts exceeded a certain amount, then the judge could leave the guidelines and go for harsher sentencing. This was a very complicated case and our wonderful lawyer knew it well.

During this time when we were going through the trial preparation, I still was not well. I had on going headaches and back pain from my car accident. Preparing for the trial probably did not help either, but God's grace is sufficient for us. He knows exactly what we need.

The big court date arrived, and we were prepared and ready. We had prayed and our wonderful prayer team was right there in the court room with us.

There was a ten-minute recess before Barry's case. We went out of the courtroom and found our lawyer. At that minute, it occurred to me that our prosecutor was not there. When I asked where he was, our lawyer told us he could not make it. **God had moved him out!** Because of this, there was a new prosecutor assigned to our case. Hallelujah!

The first thing I remember is the judge saying to my husband, "You are the most despicable thing that has ever crossed my courtroom."

I was so taken back by this pronouncement of hers. There were murderers, rapists, drug dealers, and the likes in this city that had to have come before her. I knew without a doubt this was going to be a spiritual battle over Barry's life.

First, our lawyer approached the judge and brilliantly presented his case. Then the judge called the prosecutor to come and present his case. He kept talking, but he was not making any sense. It soon became clear to everyone that he was not prepared because he kept fumbling his words and thoughts. He wasn't presenting his case with any clarity. He asked for a minute and ran to talk to someone on his team. The judge asked him to show her legally how she could throw the guidelines out. Then she would be free to pass the stiffest sentence on Barry. This new prosecutor couldn't help her. He was not prepared and there was nothing but confusion. Now she was getting agitated with him.

She was so irritated at him at this point, she asked, "Do you want to cancel this until another time when you are more prepared?"

I held my breath again and he said, "No, your Honor, I can

handle this."

He tried once again to put the pieces together, but he couldn't.

Finally, she said, "I am passing sentence on this case. I sentence you to fourteen months in prison."

She hit the gavel and it was done. The victory was ours. Barry only had to serve fourteen months and not one hundred and forty years! ***This was our miracle!*** That judge would have ruined his life over a car accident he was not responsible for and maybe a few dishonest answers to his tests. But God saw it differently. He intervened by removing the original prosecutor. God had a calling and a plan for Barry's life. It was not prison for one hundred and forty years, but freedom to live the life that God planned for him so he could fulfill his purpose and destiny!

Some of our prayer friends were crying because they thought he would not have to serve any time. I thanked them for all their love and prayers and told them I knew he would have to serve some time, but ***not one hundred and forty years***. I was rejoicing at the goodness of our God.

The enemy comes to steal, kill, and destroy, but God comes to give us life.[25] Both Barry and I were overjoyed with this outcome. Our lawyer did an excellent job and he was happy for us. We thanked him for all his love and hard work. I hope he remembers the miracle that I told him was going to happen. ***It was God who moved the prosecutor out!***

Barry and I had a few precious months together before he had to report to the work camp at Eglin Air Force base which was a white-collar prison. A dear friend of ours Barry Goldfarb, drove my husband to the Air Force base which was a wonderful gift to us. It was far away and I don't think that I could have done this. He had been sentenced to fourteen months and ended up getting an early release in ten months for good behavior. I told him he was going to the school of the Holy Ghost. He called me and told me that he was taking care of his Father's house. He was a caretaker for the grounds of a church. He was stripped of any dignity and they told him he was nothing here. Thank God he knew deep in his heart that he belonged to God.

He diligently studied the Bible and joined the Christian fellowship. They made him the president of their group. He was also there with many Jewish men and he went to their Friday night services. They all loved Barry.

He told me, "Everyone here says they are not guilty. I tell them I'm guilty and we are all sinners."

Trip to Colorado

This time was also hard for me because my daughter decided to move to Denver, Colorado. I promised her I would go with her and help her drive. She got a job working at the Denver Children's Hospital and she was excited about her move. I guess I was emotionally drained because she would drive all day and I slept. She woke me up at night when we stopped to sleep. I told her I was sorry I couldn't drive, but she understood the condition I was in.

When we got to Denver, I felt better after a few days of rest and was able to help her set up her new apartment. My husband left for prison on the same day we left for Colorado. I was saying goodbye to two very dear people in my life. Goodbyes are still very painful for me. I flew home to Orlando and got through the following months the best I could.

I visited Barry several times and to my surprise, God had me witness to some Jewish wives whose husbands were there. Barry lost a lot of weight, but he said he was feeling well. I had a word of knowledge for Barry right before he was released, and I reluctantly told him what I heard.

I said, "Honey, I know you think that when you come home this will all be over, but it will be the beginning of more things we have to go through. I don't know what all it means, but I know there is more."

I remembered the word Barry got when he was in Israel. He told the Lord he wanted to get closer to Him and God said, "You have to climb my Holy mountain." Barry was now going through the process of sanctification. The cleansing and purification were all preparation for the Holy calling and purpose for his life. The Lord was stripping and emptying Barry so He could fill him. God cannot use vessels that are not broken and yielded for the glory of God. ***There is beauty in brokenness.***

CHAPTER 10

THE LORD PROVIDES

Some friends don't help, but a true friend is closer than your own family.
-Proverbs 18:24

We thank God the Barry got an early release because of his good behavior. God is merciful and we are grateful to be the recipients of His wonderful grace.

It was exciting for me to see that we were coming to the end of this part of our journey. Barry was coming home, and we were looking forward with such anticipation to living our lives together. We went to see his former boss who told us to come see him as soon as he was released. Not only did he get Barry a job in a small hospital in South Florida, but he also gave Barry $100.00

and said, "Take your beautiful wife out to dinner."

The love of God coming through this man brought us to tears. Acts of love and kindness at a time like this you never forget! The Lord used different people for our restoration, and we are thankful for them all. Another time, a dear friend of Barry's came and gave him a significant amount of money when we were at our lowest. My son Darren also lent us some money to help us during this difficult time.

Pay Back Time

Barry started work in South Florida three days a week. He worked three twenty-four-hour shifts and then he was home for the rest of the week. Although God forgives us and takes away our guilt and shame, there are consequences for our actions. First, Barry was court-ordered to pay back Social Security restitution and fines. This was a significant amount of money, about eighty thousand dollars.

The second thing we had to deal with was the Internal Revenue Service's debt which came to about one million dollars. This amount was determined by the IRS based on the original debt plus compounded penalty fraud charges which were huge. We hired an experienced tax attorney who at one time worked for the IRS. He told us to be prepared because they are going to be tough on us.

We prayed before this IRS meeting and asked God to help us get through this with as much grace as possible. We met with the agent assigned to us and he was polite. He laid out a seven-year payment plan for us which was based on our financial situation. After we left, our lawyer told us he had never seen any meeting with his clients and the IRS go this well. This payback was a large amount of money and seven years is a longtime, but we knew that God would help us to do the righteous thing. There is that number seven again, it means completion. One thing Barry and I knew, **God is our source, and nothing is impossible for Him.**

Trust in the LORD with all your heart, and don't lean on your own understanding. In all your ways acknowledge him, and he will direct your paths.
– Proverbs 3:5-6

Be a Tither

From the time I was saved, I have always been a tither. Even though I struggled with finances and raised two children without child support, I still gave my small tithe. We must understand that the first ten percent belongs to God. It doesn't matter how much or how little we make. God must come first in our tithe and in our life. He doesn't need our money, but it was designed for us to learn to put God first. It teaches us to be givers and to be generous with whatever we have. This includes our time, talents, and our money. Even now in our desperate situation, we continued to give God the first ten percent throughout all our troubles. Our debt payments were paid monthly after our tithes. I remember one meeting with an IRS agent who told us we could not give to the church. I told him we would always give to our church because this was who we are. God comes first!

In times of great need, the worst thing you can do is hold back on tithes. You will never see God move for you if you are not faithful to His Word. God operates in the supernatural realm and He does the miraculous. Remember **He is the multiplier**. So, give Him whatever you have and then watch Him multiply and move on your behalf. It's the principle of sowing and reaping.

For example, going on a tour to Israel for twelve days and staying in good hotels with meals included costs thousands of dollars. The Lord took me on eight different trips to Israel and I only paid for two. In order for you to see these miracles working in your life, you have to believe God and be obedient to His Word. Believe me, tithing is a must for all believers.

Will a mere mortal rob God? Yet you rob me. But you ask, How are we robbing you? In tithes and offerings. You are under a curse—your whole nation—because you are robbing me. Bring the whole tithe into the storehouse, that there may be food in my house. "Test me in this," says the LORD Almighty, "and see if I will not throw open the floodgates of heaven and pour out so much blessing that there will not be room enough to store it. I will prevent pests from devouring your crops, and the vines in your fields will not drop their fruit before it is ripe," says the LORD Almighty. "Then all the nations will call you blessed, for yours will be a delightful land," says the LORD Almighty.

–Malachi 3:8-12

A Mountain of Debt

Between the three law firm bills, the tax attorney, the CPA accountants, restitution, and fines for Social Security, and the one-million-dollar IRS debt we had to pay, it was over whelming in the natural. This was a mountain of debt. Additionally, a few years later, Barry's ex-wife came against him with a judgment she had for some child support and lifetime alimony. This judgment was another million dollars. Now, the mountain of debt climbed up to two and a half million dollars! Barry was also ordered by the judge in south Florida to pay her expensive Miami attorney's bill. In all honesty, this huge amount of debt we knew we could never pay. Barry had been through another recent divorce sometime before I met him and even had his car repossessed. We had to file bankruptcy at this point and the truth is, we were a mess and broke.

We lived in an apartment and I had to go to a laundromat to clean our clothes. When Barry did work, he used my car, so I had no way to go food shopping or do errands. This was another adjustment for me. Barry was now a convicted felon just out of prison and there is a stigma that comes with that. Honestly, our trust and faith in God was literally what carried us through this difficult time. Jesus told us to live one day at a time and that is what we did. We needed a miracle from God!

Not One Penny More

We had payment plans with everyone and we faithfully paid on these debts for many years. The IRS agreement we signed and agreed to was a large amount of money we paid monthly for seven years. When we were close to the end of the seventh year, the IRS called us in for another meeting. They told us the law changed and they were going to extend our payments for three more years. The spirit of God literally rose up within me and I boldly told them we had an agreement for seven years which we faithfully paid, and we were not going to sign another agreement. Then I declared, **"You will not get one penny more."** It took us many months and meetings with other agents, but in the end we prevailed. God said, "It is enough." The seven years were complete, and we won that battle. Sometimes, we just have to stand our ground and say **not one penny more!**

We were officially released from the IRS debt and we got that release in writing. The letter they sent us had release written all over it. Years before this all happened, we had a prophetic word given to us. They said we would receive a letter from the IRS saying we were released, and the word release would be all over it. We faithfully did our part and God made sure **we were released.**

Have you noticed how many number sevens are in my testimony? That number seven means completion.

Next, we paid Social Security fines and restitution and in the right time, **we were released.**

We paid Barry's ex-wife a very large amount of money for thirteen years at which time we were notified she had passed away. This brought us **another release.** I prayed over every monthly check that was sent out to her and I can honestly say we kept our hearts clean.

We give all the glory to God for helping us over all those years to pay our debts and for setting us free. We did our part and God miraculously wiped away any remaining debt. Even a law firm who worked for us decided to forgive our debt which was about twenty-five thousand dollars, **another release.**

We did our part and God miraculously wiped away any remaining debt.

My husband worked many long hours for many years to pay on these debts. Then God said enough is enough. He brought all the releases in due season. Barry and I know we belong to God and we know He delights in us. After all of the miraculous signs and wonders He has done for us, is it any wonder why we stand in awe of Him! God took our two messed up lives and He completely transformed them into vessels of honor for His Glory. Thank You, Jesus!

In 1991, Barry worked in South Florida for nearly one year in the emergency room. Most of his patients were either Medicare or Medicaid. His boss was notified by the Social Security office that Barry, a convicted federal felon, no longer had Medicaid or Medicare privileges. These important privileges were taken away for four years. His boss at this point had no choice but to let Barry go. This was another big hurdle for us because there are very few jobs if any, where a doctor can work without these privileges.

Barry was now out of work and we were looking for God's plan in the middle of this mess. I remember sitting at our kitchen table one morning praying with Barry and suddenly I had a word of knowledge. I started to laugh, and I told Barry what the Lord was saying to us. This mountain is much too big for us to try to handle. God was going to let it all come tumbling down like the walls of Jericho.

At that time, Barry was a new believer and I had been walking with the Lord for about nineteen years. The Spirit of God was speaking and leading us in a profound way. We had many prophetic words spoken over us even before Barry went away to prison. We were thankful God sent those words of encouragement to us to help us through these difficult times. In the natural, any newly married couple would have come apart with all these troubles. But when you have God as your anchor, **it is your faith in Him** that keeps you together and helps you move forward despite all the obstacles.

Adversity and hardship will often propel you
into a much higher level of your calling and destiny.

Such are the times when you stand and watch the Lord part the waters and deliver you. Just when you think all is lost, the Lord will make a way. He is Jehovah Jireh, our provider.

Barry went on an interview for a job he found in just one small clinic. They saw very few if any Medicare or Medicaid people. His boss was a Christian woman and she gladly hired him. We were so thankful for this job. She also serviced some of the hotels at different resorts. Barry had to travel from one hotel to another and see patients. He worked this job for four years.

Family Beach Vacations

For many years, my Father and his wife Sylvia came to Florida and rented a large beach condo for two weeks. Every year, we would meet at the beach and spend time together. My sister Penny came with them and my other sister Sandy who lived here in Florida also came. We all loved the beach and it was my father's favorite place. We made many great memories during our beach vacations over the years. It is important to make memories and have quality time with our families. We looked forward to this beach get away every year.

My father loved seeing the grandchildren who were grown up and doing well. My son Darren was very close to his grandfather. They enjoyed playing shuffleboard and swimming. We all got along well and played board games or cards. Many times, we took long walks on the beach and talked about some of the funny memories we had when we were growing up. The beach is always wonderful and so refreshing. I thank God for the beautiful memories we made.

Our last beach vacation was the summer of 1991. My son brought his girlfriend with him and it was nice to meet her. She was a beautiful Christian who was tall like my son. They were a lovely couple and we enjoyed their company on that vacation. Darren always brought his surfboard to the beach. He had been surfing since he was a young teenager and even now, he still loved it.

When my son moved to the Tampa Bay area, he worked with a Christian ministry which eventually went under. He was still on fire for God and was doing Bible studies all week long. He also had a heart for young people to get saved. He decided to take over this ministry he had worked for and he made it a success. He brought top Christian groups into the Tampa Bay area and set up outdoor concerts. He worked with some great young pastors who had evangelistic hearts. Together they did some wonderful outreaches. There were a group of young people from his church who also worked with Darren and his girlfriend. I was surprised at the big-name groups he brought in, but they apparently loved what he was doing for the young people and many of them got saved.

Darren was a certified public accountant and he had great organizational skills, but even more important, he had a heart for young people who were lost. He downplayed everything he did and never took credit for anything. He was totally sold out to God. What a transformation he went through. Remember, this was my son who was such a mess in college. He was running the race for Jesus now and was totally transformed. You see, his identity had changed; he was now a disciple of Christ.

I remember about a year before he met his girlfriend, my son and I talked. He told me that he did not think he would ever get married.

I said, "Of course, you will. You will meet someone and get married."

He said, "Mom, some people are set apart for God's purposes and they never get married. I believe that I am one of them."

I felt very uneasy when I heard him talk like this. Not for a minute did I want to believe what he was saying. A year later, he was dating, and I was happy.

Colorado Wedding - March 1991

My daughter Susan had moved to Denver, Colorado after college. She was getting married to a Messianic believer. She was working at the Denver Children's hospital and loved living in Colorado. Her wedding was in early March and she was getting married at the historic Stanley Hotel high up in the mountains. We were hoping the weather would be good enough for us to be able to get there. I remember that I was crying as we drove up to the mountains to the wedding. Most people cry during the ceremony, but I was crying on the way to the wedding. We arrived at the hotel and it was in a beautiful setting. Some of our family members came to the wedding. My son Darren and her Aunt Penny were in the wedding party. Darren looked so handsome in his tuxedo. I got to dance with him at the wedding reception.

Her father had the privilege of walking her down the aisle. She was a radiant beautiful bride. They had a Messianic wedding with a string quartet playing beautiful classical music. I have to say that the view from the hotel was spectacular. We all toasted the bride and groom, and everyone had a great time. Her father, who was a concert pianist, played for the guests at the reception. It was a story book picture perfect wedding.

Christmas of 1991

Christmas of 1991 was quite different than any other I had experienced. My son told me he would not be coming home for Christmas. He was going to be with his girlfriend's family for the holidays. My newly married daughter and her husband were not coming to Florida for this Christmas either. Barry had to work long hours every week and this time of the year was always busy. Barry and I were together on Christmas day, but I had a heavy foreboding feeling that came over me which was unexplainable.

Another God Encounter- March 1992

Three months after Christmas, my daughter Susan and her husband told me they were coming to Florida on a business trip. They were going to be at a hotel in Tampa and they wanted me to come see them. She told me they were going to have dinner with my son, Darren. I talked to Barry and he encouraged me to go, but he wanted me to come home for dinner. I got in the car and as soon as I got on the highway, I started crying. The further I drove the more I cried. I could feel the Presence of God with me in the car. Soon the crying turned into sobbing which I could not control, and it made driving more difficult. I couldn't understand what was happening to me. I only knew I had never felt such anguish and sorrow.

I quickly discerned something was wrong and the Lord was giving me a warning. It was the Spirit of God taking me over once again to intercede because something very bad was going to happen. I literally cried and prayed all the way to Tampa which was a two-and-a-half-hour trip. When I arrived at the hotel, I jumped out of the car and ran inside to meet my daughter.

When she met me in the lobby, I ran and grabbed her, and asked, "Are you alright?"

She said, "Yes."

I said, "Something is very wrong somewhere. How is your husband?"

She answered, "He is in a meeting and he is fine. What is going on? Why are you so upset?"

I told her what happened to me in the car while I was driving there and she said, "It's okay, Mother. There is nothing wrong and nothing for you to worry about."

After some time passed, I calmed down and we had lunch in the restaurant. We had a nice visit and soon it was time for me to go home. Once again, she asked me to stay for dinner so I could see Darren. I told her I had to go back to Orlando because Barry wanted me home for dinner. We said our goodbyes and I got in the car and drove home. The heavy burden I felt driving there was gone. Sometimes, we do not understand the things of the Lord until after the fact. This was the case with me. Often, I am hard on myself because I think I should know more than I do.

Tom Hess and Lana

Mission Trip to Russia (April 1992)

I received a newsletter from a ministry based in Israel and I was very excited about their next mission trip to Russia. I had known the head of this ministry for years and loved the work they did. It is called Progressive Vision International. They have a House of Prayer in Jerusalem, Israel. At that time, Tom Hess was the leader. They have prayer on an ongoing basis, twenty-four hours, seven days a week. They pray for the nations of the world. He is an anointed man of God and holds meetings and conferences all over the world. Some years after this trip, Tom Hess got married. He and his wonderful wife Kate still run the ministry.

He was taking a group to Russia to pray for the release of the Jewish people. The focus for them was to be able to make Aliyah and return to Israel. This was his seventh and final trip to Russia. My spirit within me was so excited about this trip. When Barry came home from work, I gave him the newsletter to read.

After he read it, he looked at me and said, "This is your trip." I started walking around the two-mile circle in my area once each day to build up my strength for the trip. I also did some other training. I felt God was intentionally making me strong in my body.

This mission trip started in Jerusalem, Israel, where we stayed at the House of Prayer on the Mount of Olives for a few days and prayed. There were many powerful prayer warriors in this group. The first night I was there, I got ready for bed and went to sleep. I woke up a few hours later and heard a loud noise that was coming from the rooftop. I got up and went to see what was going on only to find some of our people were praying through the night. I learned there is another dimension to prayer—fasting and praying day and night. These people were on fire for God and I was honored to be with them.

We left for Russia the next day and arrived in Moscow where we stayed for a few days. This was April of 1992. This was the time when the USSR was broken up and the people were free to run their own lives. We saw people on the streets selling their wares and whatever they had.

One day, we took a taxi to a shop and we laughed because the driver was playing loud American jazz music. The buildings were so massive, they stretched for blocks long. We did see some very beautiful architectural designs, but the people we encountered were obviously struggling for simple everyday needs. There were women on the streets with babies crying and begging for money. I am sure it was a chaotic time of transition for them. In the underground subways, there were many older men who were so drunk they passed out.

We went to a church service where the young people were hanging from the rafters to hear the Word of God. Tom was friends with the pastor and his wife, and we were blessed to be with them. I remember how touched I was hearing them sing in their own language. The service was very charismatic, and Tom's sermon was powerful. These young people also met nightly in houses. We went to a house church one night and these young people were so full of love. They were eager to learn everything about Jesus. I met the woman of this house church and she showed me a music cassette tape that someone gave her in Israel. It was called "Watchmen on the Walls." She loved it and wanted to share it with me. What a small world it is. That music cassette turned out to be my recording. The church in Russia was growing, the Spirit of God was moving, and it was a beautiful sight for us to see.

We went to the biggest synagogue in Moscow on Friday night, (Shabbat). We were out on the street with our musicians playing and we sang songs of Zion. A huge crowd gathered around us to hear the music. We got to talk to some of the people about Israel. We told them they should consider leaving Moscow and make Aliyah and move to Israel while they still can. They politely listened to us, but most of them said they were comfortable there and didn't want to leave. We urged them to be careful not to stay too long as the Jews did in Germany until it was too late for them to get out.

A leader of the synagogue came out and asked why we were there. He was clearly upset, and he told us he was going to call the police to remove us. As soon as the people saw him yelling and threatening us, they all wanted to meet us and talk to us. We now had an even bigger crowd and we stayed for hours talking to everyone about the Lord and they listened. He never called the police.

We went to Odessa which is a big seaport and prayed for the Jews to be released and be able to go to Israel. We went to St. Petersburg and attended an old synagogue service and met with many people. The rabbi was very cordial, and he welcomed us to his synagogue.

I remember one Russian lady who told us she had to walk for

miles to a bus in order to get to the Synagogue. She wanted to meet us the next day, so we arranged for her to come to our hotel. She came and brought us something she had baked. We visited with her and she freely talked to us. We told her about her Messiah, Jesus and she allowed us to pray for her. It was such a tender moment because as we were praying for her, she was weeping.

"Lord, You are so (*tov*) good. You take us halfway across the world to pray for one Jewish woman who is truly seeking You."

We went to encourage a Messianic leader who Tom knew. His congregation was small, but the service was beautiful. We spent some time with them and told them we would keep them in our prayers.

We also went to a hotel where Jewish families were staying because they were leaving for Israel the next day. We sang songs of Zion to them and they loved it. We also gave them gifts and money to take with them. Most importantly, we got to pray with them. They were crying and were truly touched by our visit. It was another divine appointment. It's a privilege to be used by God.

From there we went to Romania and many of us went to orphanages to minister. The last place we traveled to was Budapest, Hungary. We stayed in a most beautiful hotel for our last night and we had a very lavish dinner. I ate a meal that night for the first time and afterwards I got sick. The food was good, but it was very rich, and I had been mostly fasting.

I talked to my husband a few times during this trip. He sounded good and he was always eager to hear about our spiritual journey.

The last few days, I started to sense something in my spirit again that made me feel very uneasy. The anointing for this trip was over for me. I did not have the heart for it anymore and I just wanted to go home. While I could not explain it, I was missing my son Darren. I wanted to go home and see him and again there was an urgency about it.

I called my husband and said, "Honey, I love you and miss you, but for some reason that I can't explain I am missing Darren. I have to get home and go to Tampa and see him."

He said, "We can certainly do that after you get home."

The last day of our mission trip, we said our goodbyes, ended our journey, and flew back to the United States of America.

CHAPTER 11

ADVERSITY AND STORMS

I was so delighted to be home and see Barry. The mission trip was powerful and very fruitful, but I was exhausted. The night I arrived home, Barry told me that one of my dearest Messianic friends had passed away while I was in Russia. He did not want to tell me while I was away. I was so tired I remember only a few tears ran down my face. She was such a wonderful woman of God and I am sure the Lord welcomed her into Heaven. The next day I wanted to get in a car and go to Tampa to see my son. Barry was concerned about me because he thought I needed to rest.

He said, "Why don't you call Darren and see if he can come to see you?"

I called Darren and we had a long conversation on the phone. I asked him how he was doing? He told me he was good, and work was going well. I told him that I had to see him, and he said he and his girlfriend could drive to Orlando over the weekend to see us.

He said, "Sunday is Mother's Day and we can be together."

I agreed to this alternative arrangement. Barry and I had previous plans to go to a conference at the Carpenters Home Church in Lakeland, Fla. We were planning to be there for two days and then be home for Mother's day weekend. This conference was focused on prayer and deliverance.

We arrived on May 6, 1992 and stayed at a hotel down the street from the church. After the evening service was over, we went to our hotel. The next day, May 7, we were at the church all day going to different sessions. After the morning session, the speaker was giving prophetic words to different people.

He came to me and gave me this word: "*'**Wisdom is going to grow in your life like a tree of life. A new impartation of strength and glory. Get ready. It's coming up like a fountain, a burst of new wine. A tree of wisdom is being erected in your life,' God says to tell you.***"

Some of my friends came running over to me and said, "You got such a wonderful word."

I said, "Yes, and I wonder what I have to go through to get it."

We went to the evening session and it started with corporate worship. We were in the middle of a worship song when suddenly, one of the leaders stopped the worship and said, "We have to pray because someone's child is in trouble."

The Lord spoke to him and told him we had to stop everything and pray. He said, "Prayer is essential because this was very serious." I told Barry, "Susan is married and I'm going to pray for Darren." We prayed for everyone's children, and when that was done, we continued with the service. After the evening service was over, we went back to our hotel and went to sleep.

Very early in the morning, the phone rang and woke us up. Barry answered the phone and I went to the bathroom. When I came back into the room, I heard Barry talking very quietly on the phone to his daughter and he was crying. I climbed on the bed and put my arms around him to hug him because I thought the call had something to do with his adopted son who was always in trouble.

He turned to me and said, "It is I who need to be consoling you. It is your son Darren who has died in a car accident tonight."

O my God, those are words that a parent never wants to hear. I remember I was crying so hard. I do not think anyone could have helped me in that moment, not even Barry who I loved dearly. I ran into the bathroom sobbing and I cried out to God to help me with this pain that was so deep. I wondered how this happened and why; I needed some answers. As I was praying and crying, a peace came flooding over me and I heard the Lord tell me to pull myself together. He said He would lead me and be with us through it all.

I washed my face and went back to the bedroom very calmly and told Barry that I wanted to go to Tampa and see my son. Barry called the hospital and found out that he was at the medical examiner's office. Barry called them and they told him people were not allowed to come there, but because Barry was a doctor, they told us we could come. In a matter of minutes, I threw everything in a suitcase, got dressed, and we were on our way to Tampa. I knew I had to stay calm because I wanted to understand what happened.

When we got to the medical examiner's office, they were very kind and did everything they could to help us. They gave us an office so we could be alone and make some necessary phone calls.

They promised me that I could see my son, but only through a glass. I remember going through two doors and I saw him behind a glass lying on a table covered with a sheet. All I could see was his face. Within a second of seeing my son, I heard this loud rush of noise coming from the front office. I turned and looked through the doors and saw his girlfriend and all his friends. They were sobbing. At that very moment, I felt the overwhelming love of Jesus. I turned away from my son and walked out the door to help his friends who had been up all night at the hospital. They were understandably distraught and exhausted from this tragic event. My heart went out to these faithful friends he loved so much. I put my arms around them, and we were all on the floor in a heap, hugging each other and crying together. This was such a bittersweet moment; one I will never forget.

At that very moment, I felt the overwhelming love of Jesus.

They calmed down enough to tell us what happened. Early in the evening, Darren was on his way to see his girlfriend. He came to an intersection that had no light. As he was turning into that street, a large sports truck hit him and spun his car around. His girlfriend, who only lived two blocks away, heard the crash and she sent her sister down the street to see if it was Darren. She said he was late, and he was never late. She was sure it was him.

A few minutes later, her sister came running back to the house in a state of panic and told her it was Darren's car. The police told them they helicoptered him to Tampa General Hospital which has a major trauma center. All his friends got in their cars and headed to the hospital to pray and wait for the doctor's results.This accident happened early in the evening, right about the time we were called to pray at the conference for someone's child who was in serious trouble. The doctors in the trauma center worked very hard to save Darren's life because he was so young. They could not stop the massive bleeding because many of his major organs were torn in two. My husband who is a doctor, assured me that he was unconscious long before he died.

God of Mercy and Grace, receive your child into your Heavenly place. He ran the race with all of his strength and crossed the finish line. Well done my precious son, you are God's champion. A prophet told me, "Darren received a martyr's crown."

God's ways are not our ways, for as high as the Heavens are from the earth that's how high His ways are. One thing I know, God is Sovereign and even in tragic situations that we don't understand, we can be sure that He is working all things together for our good, for those who are called according to His purposes.

We asked Darren's girlfriend and friends to help us with urgent things that had to be done. They were not only willing, but they were a real blessing to us. We did not know our way around Tampa, and we needed to go to many different places including our son's townhouse. I also wanted to go see his car and the truck that hit him because I wanted to discern what happened. We went to the place where they towed the cars. His brand-new car was hit so hard it was absolutely totaled. As I looked at my son's car, I was literally shaking because I realized just how violent this collision was that took his life. I opened the door and saw his glasses lying on the floor. I took them and the man who worked there said you cannot take anything out of his car. I said, "You don't understand, my son needs his glasses." He looked at me for a moment and then walked away.

The truck that hit Darren's car had satanic stickers with skulls and crossbones all over it. There were many empty beer cans inside and there was hardly any damage done to the truck. I never doubted that the spiritual battle was raging, and the enemy took my son's life.

However, I was puzzled as to why the Lord stopped the conference that night with such urgency and had us pray. Much later, I came to understand that God called us to pray at that specific time, so my son could be released to go home to his Heavenly Father. The plan of the enemy was to keep him alive in a vegetative state, so the enemy could use this to tell young people, "This is what you get for serving the Lord." My son never wanted to be kept alive like that. This is exactly what he told his sister and me the last "Best Christmas Ever" we spent together in Colorado.

At this time, I suddenly remembered him telling me he didn't think he would ever be married. He said, "Some people are set apart for the Lord." I did not want to hear it at the time, but now I realized he was right. That was a prophetic word given to him by God. I also remembered the trip I made to Tampa to see my daughter in March, and the encounter I had with God. Looking back on it now, I know the Lord was trying to give me one last time to be with my son. God knows everything and that is why it is critical that we learn to hear His voice and follow His lead.

I have learned that when the Holy Spirit is speaking to us whether it's in a dream, a vision, or an encounter like the one I had in the car, we must listen and be obedient. This was not an ordinary encounter I had with God. The spirit of God was giving me an urgent message about something bad that was going to happen.

I should have listened to my daughter who tried to get me to stay and have dinner with my son who lived in Tampa. She asked me to stay twice, and both times I said no, I have to go home.

That dinner my daughter and her husband had with my son that night was the last time any of us saw him. Later my daughter showed me the last picture that was taken of my son that night, and in the background of this picture was a hospital. I asked her what hospital was this? She said "It's the Tampa General hospital which has one of the best major trauma centers."

Ironically, it turned out to be the same hospital my son died in just six weeks later. I found it tragic that his life was cut off at the young age of twenty-seven.

The biggest lesson I learned is that I should have listened to the voice of God. I don't believe the outcome would have changed, but the Lord was urging me to stay and see my son. It all became so clear to me; I should have stayed.

Listening and obeying God's Voice will always be my first choice!

I regret that I did not listen to the voice of God and decided to go home. That was a very painful lesson that I learned. Hopefully we learn from our mistakes.

Later, I found out that Tampa at that time was the heavy metal capital of the world. In the supernatural realm, Darren was coming up against some giant forces of darkness. The ministry he was leading was called the "Upper Room Ministry." He brought in the top Christian groups of that day to do these public outdoor concerts designed to win souls. Many of Darren's friends and co-workers asked me what do we do now? I told them they should do what Darren did, win souls.

We took his girlfriend home to Orlando with us because she wanted to leave that area. She was very fragile and wanted to be with our family at this time. She was overcome with grief and exhaustion. At some point, she told me she wanted to die and go be with Darren.

I told her, "That is not the plan of God for you. You will live and you will go on and have a full productive life." She was frail and emotionally drained, and the truth is so was I. My daughter Susan was able to love on her and minister to her. Our whole family loved her, and I was grateful for all their help.

Barry notified our family and together they made airline and hotel reservations so they could be here for Darren's funeral. This was Mother's Day weekend, and here I am making funeral arrangements for my son.

I got a call from some young pastors from California who knew Darren and had worked with him in ministry. They were shocked and sad to hear the news and asked if they could come to Florida and do his memorial service.

I said, "Please come, that would be wonderful."

Even in the depths of my grief, I saw the Lord orchestrating everything. I was on empty going through the motions of whatever had to be done. Everything was overwhelming for me, but the Spirit of God was near. I remember telling everyone in my family that no one should be blaming God for the accident.

The first thing I had to do was forgive the young man who borrowed the truck from a friend and hit Darren's car that night. I prayed that he would get saved and find Jesus. He was just a young man in college who was in a hurry that night. The Bible says the rain falls on the just and the unjust. We live in a fallen world and even though we are believer's, bad things do happen.

I got a call from some people who lived in the neighborhood where the accident happened. They were sorry to hear about my son. They said accidents happened at this intersection almost every week. For years they tried to get a light put up, but now that my son died, they felt I could help them get that light installed.

I said, "Yes, I will help any way I can."

Later, I was told they got the light installed and they thanked me and said they were praying for us. Hopefully, no one else will ever die at that intersection.

Darren worked at a very large insurance company in Tampa at the time of his death. They had to get grief counselors for their young workers who worked with him. He had started the first Bible study at this insurance company. The Bible study doubled in size after his death and his boss told me they named it after Darren. The owners of the company called me and told me how much they liked my son. They said he was brilliant, and they were sure he would rise to the top of the company. They came to his funeral and many of the young people he worked with also came. I received so many letters and cards from people Darren had helped. They were so touched by him and his generous heart. He was a giver and always gave God the glory!

I had my son's girlfriend staying with us and I promised the Lord I would take care of her as she went through the grief process. We all had to help her get through this so she could live the life God planned for her.

Some of my family came from Pennsylvania. I felt sorry for my Dad who was older and not in good health. He was close to Darren over the years and he was really struggling with his death. We heard that many young people from Tampa were coming to the funeral, so we decided to have a luncheon for all the people who came from out of town.

The day of Darren's memorial service, the young pastors came from California and led the service. They were powerful and talked a lot about his desire to see young people come to the Lord. Our dear friend whose wife passed away while I was in Russia, got up and read a letter he received from Darren just a few weeks earlier. In this letter, Darren said many kind things about his wife, but he also said, **"We all need to be right with the Lord because at any time, he could be calling us home. We never know when our time here is up." How prophetic! The Lord called Darren home three weeks later.**

Hearing our friend read Darren's letter was heart wrenching for me. He certainly had insight about how fragile life is. The young pastors invited people to come forward and give their lives to Jesus just as Darren had. There were many young people who answered that call. In his short life, he helped many young people find Jesus. Even after he died, young souls were won for Christ at his memorial service. My Jewish father was sitting in the front row and I was praying some of this would help him see his need for Jesus (Yeshua), our Jewish Messiah.

After the service, we had a luncheon for the family and for those who came from out of town. It was held at a small country club nearby and the people who worked there were very gracious. My father was walking around looking very perplexed and I asked him what is wrong? He said, "I don't understand how someone so young could touch so many people in such a short time." Darren was twenty-seven years old at the time of his death.

I did not know that Darren had written his grandfather a letter before he died. He told him he loved him very much and that was why he was writing to tell him about Jesus. He basically told him he wanted him to get saved before it was too late. He presented the gospel message to him in a very loving way.

After Darren died, a prophet told me he saw my father reading a letter. He said he was reading it over and over. My son was such an evangelist. His sister also has the same heart for lost souls. My daughter Susan went through deep grief at the death of her brother. She was wise enough to go for grief counseling after she returned home. It was very hard for her because they were only two years apart and very close most of their lives. She did many kind things for him even in college. He had a great sense of humor and he was a loving son and brother, a gift to us all.

He had a great sense of humor and he was a loving son and brother, a gift to us all.

The week after the Memorial service, I got up at church and

did one worship song. I was very weak and could hardly stand, but this was something I had to do. I wanted to send a message to the enemy that he was not going to stop me from fulfilling my destiny. In fact, I was more determined than ever to do even greater works for God. One thing I knew, God was taking Barry and I to a higher place, to another level. We were going through the refiner's fire and one thing I do know is that God uses everything in our lives to do a work in us. In times of adversity we can see God more clearly. His strength is made perfect in our weakness, because our need for Him is so much greater. I heard a pastor say, there is no smell of smoke when you come out of the fire. The only fragrance is JESUS! To God be all of the Glory.

Settling the Estate

Over the next few months, I had to take care of all the legal parts of Darren's estate. He left his sister and me his insurance money. We were the three musketeers. I had to go to Tampa many times to make arrangements for the sale of his townhouse. After we removed his furniture and his belongings, a dear friend of mine Jett went with me to help me clean and prepare it to be sold.

I walked into his place one day and felt water on the carpet going upstairs. His air conditioner unit was there, and I knew it was leaking. I called the phone number on the unit and told the man the problem I was having. He told me that he heard that my son had died, and he was so sorry. He told me that my son helped his nephew find Jesus and was having Bible studies with him. He came to my sons place and fixed the air conditioner. He told me my son was so wonderful he would not take any money for the work he did.

You see, when I found the leaking air conditioner unit, I could only see the problem. The Lord not only wanted me to get it fixed, but He wanted me to hear that wonderful testimony about my son and this man's beloved nephew. My son was busy doing his Heavenly Father's kingdom business right to the end.

I remember he planted a tree in his backyard, and it was not looking good. I watered his new tree every time I went there and still it was dying. One day, I became angry and I went out to the tree and hit it with a broom. Here I am in his backyard yelling at the tree to live. I was desperately wanting something of his to live. I am sure this anger was part of the grief process I was experiencing. I don't know if the tree lived or died, but the townhouse sold very quickly because some wonderful realtors got the word out about my son. They knew I lived in Orlando and I needed to sell his townhouse right away.

Emotionally, it was very hard for me to be in his home. A part of me thought I was fixing up his townhouse so he could come back. I said my last goodbye the day the townhouse sold and reality set in. I signed papers, turned over his keys, and cried all the way home to Orlando. God knew I needed to bring closure to his estate so I could go home and start to heal.

I had to stop looking back, I had to move forward, but that was easier said than done. A pastor's wife who also lost her son years ago told me you cannot drive a car looking in the rear-view mirror. That says it all. Someone else told me time heals all wounds. That is not exactly true. Time allows you to move into the acceptance stage of the grief. The deep pain does diminish with time, but the loss is always there. Yes, every child is unique and irreplaceable. However, having said all that, I am thankful for the time we all had with him. I do not have enough words to say how grateful I am that he gave his life back to God in college. I know that without a doubt Darren is in Heaven with His Messiah and that gives me peace.

Spiritual Retreats

I took my son's girlfriend to two Christian retreats. We needed to get some rest and be filled with the Word of God. Everyone was wonderful and many gave us words from the Lord which were uplifting and encouraging. She needed this time because she had to start school in the Fall. Our family loved her, and we wanted her to have the very best life. At one conference we went to, she was given a prophetic word that in exactly one year, she would meet her husband. She would be the mother of several children and they would have a good life. This word did come true to the exact timing.

Throughout this sad time, I cried tears of grief. The grief would come in waves and I never knew when it would happen. Honestly, anything could set it off. I woke up one morning and turned to my husband and said, "Let's go see Darren in Tampa today."

He said, "Honey, don't you remember that Darren has passed away and has gone to Heaven?"

"Oh, yes," I said sadly.

The strong will to see your child again does tricks to your mind. The grieving process is important to go through. It is the only way you can move on and live your life to the fullest. It does take time, and no one can tell you how long. I thank God I had faith to help me through it. A few people came to me and said some awful things during this time.

One Christian lady said, "You will know you are over it when you don't remember his birthday."

"Really?"

The best thing you can do is pray for people who are going through grief. We do not grieve like people without any hope, but let me tell you, it is the deepest pain any mother and father will ever go through. Burying your child is just not natural.

Lord give us a sensitivity and teach us how to minister to people who are going through deep suffering and loss. Grieving takes time; it is a process.

God was kind to me and gave me new friends that prayed for me daily. They lived in another town and heard about my loss. We became very close over the years and I thank God for my praying friends.

My daughter Susan called me in the Fall of 1992 and told me she thought she was pregnant. When I was unresponsive, she asked me what is wrong? I started to cry and told her that I could not bear one more disappointment.

She said, "I understand, and I will go for the test."

A few days later she called me back and said, "I am pregnant."

This was such good news, the first sign of new life for our family.

After the funeral was over and everyone had gone home, reality set in. I was blessed to have God walk me through this hard time because this was the worst year of my life! I had physical pain from my car accident and deep emotional pain from the loss of my son.

In February of 1993, I was invited to minister at a church in South Florida. We were getting ready and I bent over to put my stockings on, and I felt a stabbing pain go up my back. I screamed and broke out in a sweat. My husband checked me out, but the pain had left. I was a bit shaken, but it went away. We got in the car and drove onto the highway heading for South Florida. The stabbing pain had returned. I knew I had to get to the hospital immediately. I told my husband to get off the road quickly and take me to the nearest emergency room. We saw the doctor and they gave me a shot for the severe pain. They scheduled me for a CT scan and in the meantime, I was put on major pain medicine. The pain level was a number ten. I prayed that I would not become a drug addict.

After persistent excruciating pain for over a month, I ended up having surgery for a herniated disc. A part of the disc broke off and was pressing on the nerve root and that is why it was so painful. I thank God that I was able to have that surgery. This was my time for great healings of body, soul, and spirit.

As I was recuperating from my surgery, I spoke to my older sister Rae many times by phone. She was feeling terrible and crying for me because of the loss of my son. My sister was suffering with major heart disease and in April of 1993, eleven months after my son died, she also died. She was a strong believer and went home to be with her Heavenly Father. I was sad because I was not able to go to her funeral. I was still recovering from my back surgery. I have very fond memories of my sister Rae who use to babysit us when my parents went out. She took good care of us and made the best fudge.

Then in 1994, my brother-in-law also passed away. He had a very bad heart condition and had been on oxygen for years.

In January of 1995, my sister Penny called me to tell me that my father who had cancer was dying. I went home to Pennsylvania to see him. As I sat visiting with him, he talked about how much he missed my son Darren. I told him we all missed him, but my peace came from knowing he was with the Lord in Heaven. I remember my father's doctor came to the house to see him and he said, "Fred, you are going to meet your maker soon and his name is Jesus." I went back to Florida and within a few days, my father died. I don't know if my father ever accepted Jesus (Yeshua) as his Jewish Messiah. I can only hope he did.

In May of 1998, I was on the worship team of a fiftieth anniversary celebration of the state of Israel. I was in my hotel when I got the call saying my beautiful sister Sandy, who was only sixty years old, had a massive heart attack and died. We were only two years apart growing up and we were always very close. She was a beautiful believer and a wonderful Bible teacher. Everybody loved her and I am sure she is in Heaven with the lover of her soul, Jesus. She has a daughter Emi who has a family and they live in Philadelphia. She also has a son who is an artist and also lives in Philadelphia. We see them when we can and try to stay in touch. We miss their mother who was my very dear sister and friend. From 1992 to 1998, we buried five of my immediate family members. This included my son who died first. The path of suffering is part of the journey we are on. I prayed that the past seven years of our lives would somehow be used for God's glory. I never felt so close to God as I did when I was going through those difficult times. Barry and I were also going through all his legal battles during these same seven years. Honestly, I was a wreck much of the time. Barry was working long hours so we could pay our two and a half million-dollar debts. It was only by the grace of God that we were we able to keep going and come out victorious.

The path of suffering is part of the journey we are on.

I have learned that in our weakness He is strong, He is my hiding place. To live for Jesus is our highest goal, but it is not easy. During this time of grief, I could feel God's presence hovering over me. I could not sleep at night because that's when we got the call about my son's accident. I was up many nights praying and I could sense His presence. This was a time of deep intimacy with Him like I had never known, but at the same time it was painful. I was so empty and yet so close to my Savior.

I have learned if you are ever going to do anything significant for the Kingdom of God you will face many battles. You must know who your enemy is and how to take your God-given authority and stand against him. He comes to steal, kill, and destroy. Jesus came to give us abundant life.

We will go through the fiery furnace at some point in our lives. God is refining us, testing and trying us. He is molding us into vessels of silver and gold for His use. He is the potter and we are the clay. Our faith in God has to be our anchor and we must live by faith. Without faith it is impossible to please God. Signs and miracles will follow those who put their trust in the Lord.

Barry and I have been greatly tried and tested throughout those seven years and beyond. God wants our lives to be a living testimony to His faithfulness.

We are overcomers by the blood of the Lamb and by the word of our testimony.

New Beginnings (The Faithfulness of God)

During this time, we were still battling legal issues concerning Medicare/Medicaid privileges. Once again, we needed a lawyer and a miracle. I called many law firms who turned us down because we didn't have money for a retainer.

Then I called one more law firm and this female lawyer listened to me and said, "Lana, I will take the case."

It turns out she was a Christian and had a beautiful heart. She took our case with no money down for a retainer and helped us with the legal battles. At this point, I was so relieved, I was crying.

She said to me, "This difficult time will pass, and you and your husband will have a life."

Such words of wisdom! At this point, I could not think about any future for us, but she was right. This was a season of our lives and we would get through it by God's grace.

We paid this lawyer monthly payments for several years. Her law firm contacted us many years later and told us every year they voted on forgiving a client's debt. This year they decided to forgive our debt which was about $25,000.00. What a wonderful gift to us! They said we were so faithful to pay through all the years, they wanted us to be released. ***Thank You Lord for another release.***

Three Interviews (*Look for the favor of God*)

In 1995, the Federal government reinstated Barry's Medicare and Medicaid privileges. Barry had three interviews to go on and I told him to look for the favor of God. At each interview, he was upfront with the fact that he was a convicted felon, served his time, and was now restored. The first two job interviewers told him no thank you.

The third interview was quite different. This man listened to Barry and said, "God forgives, doesn't He? It would be an honor to have you work for us." Barry's credentials were beyond excellent. This man who interviewed him was a man of great faith. We believe that he was chosen by God to help us. This godly man and others became a large part of Barry's restoration. We had been given a prophetic word prior to this interview that said, "The Lord is giving you a job and it may not be what you would choose, but it will be like an umbrella (a covering). Long after everyone is gone, you will still be there." This prophetic word has come to pass. Barry has worked for the same wonderful employer for the past twenty-five years. His employer has been a wonderful covering and a blessing to us, and Barry has been a dedicated and outstanding worker.

Once again, we see the absolute faithfulness of our God. He is Jehovah Jireh, our provider.

One of the most important things I have learned is to praise God through the good times and the bad. He is God and He is always worthy of our praise. We can't see the battles that are going on in the supernatural realm, but the dark forces are at work all the time. Just know that God is with us, He is for us, and He is making sure that we reach our destiny. Remember that nothing takes God by surprise.

Through it all, I can honestly say that God has taught me to trust Him in an even greater way. I know that I'm nothing without Him, but I am more than victorious by the power of God at work in me. We can do all things through Christ who strengthens us.

In love I would like to say that we must be careful not to bring God down to our level. We need to see God for who He truly is. It is an awesome and fearful thing to be in the throne room of God. Revelation 4:3-11 describes God seated on His throne in all His brilliance. Read this and linger here for a while…

> *There is a rainbow round about His throne like unto an emerald. And round about the throne were four and twenty seats; and upon the seats I saw four and twenty elders sitting, clothed in white raiment, and they had on their head's crowns of gold. And out of the throne proceeded flashes of lightning and thundering's and voices; and there were seven lamps of fire burning before the throne, which are the seven spirits of God. And before the throne there was a shiny sea of glass sparkling like crystal; in the center and around the throne were the four living beings, each covered with eyes, front and back. The first of these living beings was like a lion; the second was like an ox; the third had a human face; and the fourth was like an eagle in flight. Each of these living beings had six wings, and their wings were covered all over with*

eyes inside and out. Day after day and night after night they keep on saying "Holy, Holy, Holy is the Lord God almighty who was, who is, and who is to come." Whenever the living beings give Glory and honor and thanks to Him who sits on the throne forever and ever, the twenty- four elders fall down and worship Him. And they lay their crowns before the throne and say, "You are worthy O Lord our God to receive glory and honor and power. For you have created all things, and for your pleasure they are and were created."

I've learned not to limit God because, **HE IS LIMITLESS.**

CHAPTER 12

OUT OF THE ASH HEAP

THE BIRTH OF MINISTRY

In the Fall of 1990, Barry taught on the Biblical Feasts in our small church. This was the first time I saw Barry's wonderful teaching gift. His teaching was very good, but I thought it would be an even better presentation if we added some Messianic music and dance to it. We both agreed this would make the celebration more exciting. My giftings were in the arts and worship. Remember, I had gone to Juilliard School of Music in New York as a dance major. I was also a professional singer for many years before I got saved. After my salvation, I sang in our church choir and with different worship teams. Barry and I were also part of a Messianic congregation for a few years and I was on their worship team as well.

Music was what I loved all my life, but worshipping God took me to a whole new level. I found this to be the ultimate experience. In simple terms, the difference between doing music and worship is one word, **anointing**. After my son died, I met and spent time with a worship leader whose name is Claren McQueen. He was the worship leader with the International Christian Embassy in Jerusalem (ICEJ). I sang in many outreaches we did for Israel and he was the worship leader. There was something different about Claren. It wasn't just about the good music he did, but more importantly, it was about the intimate relationship he had with God.

An intimacy and closeness with God will spill over into everything you do. I pray the Spirit of God who dwells in us will take us into the Holy of Holies, the place of His Presence. He is the God of all creation, He made the stars and the constellations, He is Majestic and Holy, clothed in splendor and glory and He is an all-consuming fire. Let us come to Him in humility and worship Him for who He is. ***Lord, help us to lift our eyes and our hearts upward and see You seated in Heavenly places on Your Throne.***

We cannot be satisfied with just going through life the same way we always did.

We cannot be satisfied with just going through life the same way we always did. We have the Holy Spirit (*Ruach ha Kodesh*) living in us, and we are empowered and anointed to go and do great things for the Kingdom of God. Over the years, I have become a worshipper of the Most High God (*El Elyon*). I sit at my piano and worship the Lord. Sometimes, I just get lost in Him. He takes me to another place in the spiritual realm and it's a beautiful anointed experience. My audience is God my Father.

During my times of worship, I make sure all the portals are closed except the portal of Heaven. I turn off all noise and distractions that would interfere with my time with God. He must be my one and only focus. I have grown so much over the year's by spending precious time with God in prayer and worship. When you are in this place, He will speak to you. I personally have never heard an audible voice of God. What I have heard is God speaking to me in a small still voice.

Sometimes He gives me information that I had no knowledge of before. It's like He downloads it in my brain and out comes information that even takes me by surprise when it comes out of my mouth. The Spirit of God may give you a word of knowledge, or some encouragement, or direction. For me, it's often a word of knowledge or a prophetic word. Very often, He speaks to me through the message in a song.

The Bible says ***as we draw near to God, He will draw near to us.*** Let us come before Him with a pure heart desiring to have fellowship with Him. The Lord has been pursuing us since the dawn of time and now is the time for us to pursue Him. Let's run after Him with all of our hearts and give Him the honor and glory due His name because ***we were created to worship Him!***

The Birth of the Feast of Tabernacles

In 1991, we decided to do a small celebration of The Feast of Tabernacles. I taught some of our people how to do some Hebraic circle dances and they danced to wonderful Messianic music. They wore white skirts and blouses and we put royal blue sashes around their waists. Barry did the teaching and it was good (*tov*). The response was wonderful, and everyone loved it.

At this point, the birth of our ministry looked very small and insignificant, but we saw it as a wonderful opportunity to teach the church about their Biblical Hebraic roots. We knew this was our calling and we felt honored to be doing the Lord's work. We have also done many Passover Seders in many different churches over the years. Passover is another great teaching showing the symbolism of the blood over the doorposts of each Jewish household. It was the saving grace and deliverance for Israel after four hundred years of slavery in Egypt and its fulfillment was in Jesus, the Passover lamb.

A Prophetic Word

In the summer of 1992, just months after my son's death, Barry and I went to see the house my daughter and her husband bought in Evergreen, Colorado. This quaint town was about forty-five minutes from downtown Denver. It was a lovely home high up in the mountains with beautiful trees everywhere. Early in the morning, Barry was outside praying on their beautiful deck wearing his prayer shawl and he had a prophetic word from the Lord. He told me the Lord said he was giving me a child. The truth is I laughed just like Sarah did in the Bible and I told Barry this cannot be true because I am past the age of childbearing.

I said, "You must mean our daughter Susan will have a child."

At this point, I could see that Barry was upset with me and he said, "I don't care what you say, I heard the Lord say He is giving you a child and you are taking care of this child."

The birth of our first grandchild came on July 3, 1993. My daughter had a baby girl and they named her Elizabeth Anna. She was the first sign of new life in our family. The name Elizabeth means consecrated to God. I made it to the hospital just in time to be there when she was born. After many long hours in labor, the doctors decided my daughter had to have a cesarean section. Because of this operation, she could not lift anything for six weeks, not even her baby.

She needed help, and I was glad that I was there. Her husband was helpful, but he had to go back to work in downtown Denver. I stayed with them during this time and took care of my daughter and the new baby. It was a three-level house and the washer and dryer were in the bottom level. This was about two and a half months after my major back surgery. Only by God's grace was I able to be there and help.

At this moment, it occurred to me that the word that Barry spoke to me about a year before was true. God did bring a child into our family through my daughter and her husband, and because of their circumstances, she needed my help. Here I was taking care of this child and her mother in the exact same place where Barry received that prophetic word almost one year ago. You see God's plan will unfold with or without us believing it because, He is God.

A few months later, my daughter had to be operated on again for damage to her chest and upper body because of the car accident she had a year ago. The surgeon wanted to wait until after she gave birth. I went back to Denver again to help her and take care of Elizabeth. Her husband was home on the weekends and at night and that was a real blessing. I was still going through the grief process and was restless and sleepless much of the night. Barry was working long hours during this time and, of course, I really missed him. It was clear to me that Barry was doing what he had to do, and I was called here to help my daughter and her husband. Children are gifts from God and they certainly bring joy into our lives, but I was still going through the grieving process.

My grief was delayed because I had to take care of so many things. The funeral arrangements, my son's estate, the cleaning, and ultimate sale of his townhouse. I had to make sure his girlfriend was well enough to go on to the next phase of her life. My son previously told me that he was looking at rings because he wanted to get engaged. She was doing as well as anyone could, but this was a tragic loss for her, and healing would take some time. I went with her when she moved to Memphis, Tennessee where she was going to school to become an optometrist. She got moved and settled into her apartment and we prayed this season in her life would be the new beginning she needed. We kept in close touch by phone and we had many people praying for her as she made this hard transition in her life. The word of prophecy she received at one of the conferences we went to came true. She met a wonderful young Christian man in school. They dated and got married and had three wonderful children. They both worked hard and are very successful in their own business. We keep in touch at Christmas time, by sending pictures and newsy letters. I am so happy for the wonderful Godly family the Lord has given her. Once again, we see the faithfulness of God.

Returning to my sharing about our ministry. It wasn't until after my son's death in 1992 that big changes came. The Lord led us to a much larger church where they welcomed us and the ministry and it began to grow. Barry and I had very little money to live on or spend because of the mountain of debt we had to pay. After my son's death, I inherited a sum of money which I used to birth the ministry God gave us. Isn't it interesting how God brought finances into our lives at the same time we were birthing a ministry He has called us to do?

One precious seed, my son, goes into the ground and out of the ash heap of our lives, comes this anointed Feast of Tabernacles.

Who can tell what God will do or when He will call us to do it? In the natural, I would never have wanted to start any ministry after going through so much pain and sorrow. But God's ways are not our ways. He knows what is best and God's timing is always perfect. My husband and I were sanctified, empty, yielded vessels that God wanted to use for His purposes.

The Lord often uses ordinary people who have messed up their lives as Barry and I did before we were saved. Some of the disciples failed the Lord in different ways and at different times, and yet, they were called to a very high calling. They were called and chosen just as you and I are called and chosen for God's purposes. We are new creations in Jesus (Yeshua), and as we surrender our lives to Him, His plan and purposes will unfold in our lives.

When you absolutely know you cannot do it on your own, your need for God is so much greater.

The Feast of Tabernacles

In Exodus 25:8 God said, "Let them make me a sanctuary; that I might dwell among them."

God desires to have times of intimacy and fellowship with us. We were made to have fellowship with Him and because I am a worshipper, I wanted this Feast of Tabernacles to be an extravagant offering to our God. I prayed that God's people would be immersed in His Holy presence. A good worship leader will be able take people into the presence of God.

Zechariah 4:6 says, "It's not by might, nor by power, but by my spirit saith the Lord of Hosts."

The Lord guided and directed us to make the Holy things for

this Tabernacle Celebration. We were aware that this Feast was a time of joy and celebration, but it was also a time of communion and intimacy with God, and He is Holy, Holy, Holy.

In Exodus 25, the Lord directed the skilled artists to build everything for the tabernacle.

The Lord brought us all sorts of skilled and talented people to make all the artifacts needed for this ministry. Skilled singers, musicians, and dancers, skilled seamstresses, banner makers, banner carriers, and priests of the Most High God.

Artists and Feast Preparations

Costumes were designed and made for our dance team and all the extras. They were beautiful and colorful, but also modest. The priest robes and hats were made. The high priest robe and undergarments were sewn and done according to biblical specifications. The high priest ephod (breast plate) and his hat were made by a pastor's wife, Charlotte Brown. She felt honored that she was chosen to make these holy garments.

We met Lin Giard, who has a ministry of nations costumes. She designed and made each piece and they are used for different ministries. She has graciously let us use these beautiful nations costumes throughout all of the years. We have also been given some lovely nations costumes by several people who have been to the nations. Lin was also a part of our dance team for years. The visual of these costumes and the music with the dancers and extras dressed in these garments is absolutely stunning! This visual shows the blood of Jesus (*Yeshua*) was shed for all people, from every tribe and every tongue, and every nation throughout the whole earth.

The altar of incense was constructed according to the measurements in scripture. Then the Ark of the Covenant was designed and made with the cherubim on the lid. All these artifacts were made according to biblical measurements.

It is a certainty when you are doing any ministry for the Lord there will be spiritual battles, especially a worship ministry. The Lord has taught me to persevere no matter how many obstacles we must overcome. Barry and I have learned to trust the Lord in all things. The birth of this ministry was not easy, but we knew in our hearts it was the Lord. The cherubim were sculptured by an artist who worked at Disney in Orlando area and they turned out beautiful. The same woman who made the cherubim, told me she could do gold gilding. I did not know anything about gilding, but I soon found out how costly and expensive it was. However, not everything went right during this process. She called me a week later and confessed that she had

The Lord has taught me to persevere no matter how many obstacles we must overcome.

never done gold gilding before, and it did not turn out well. That was an understatement. When she showed them to me, I thought this was a disaster, and the beautiful cherubim were ruined.

She gave me the name and phone number of a man who was a master gold gilder and wrote the book on gold gilding, but he lived in New York. God was with us because this man just happened to be in the Orlando area at this exact time, because he was recuperating from an operation. It became very clear to me that God was once again orchestrating everything just as He did so many times in our lives. He was bringing us the very best artists to help us put this Feast of Tabernacles together for His glory. When the gilding expert came to see the cherubim, he told us that all of the gold gilding had to be carefully removed. He told us this process would be a slow and tedious task. The cost of this work was expensive, but we wanted the best for the Lord. Weeks later, he finished his work and we were delighted to see the new gilded cherubim. They were radiant gold and beautiful. We paid him and thanked him for graciously doing this special project.

The altar of incense was an easier task. It was made from wood and then painted with special gold paint by another talented artist in the Orlando area. We were blessed to have some of the finest artists living here because they either worked for Disney or for Universal Studios.

When we did a Feast of Tabernacles in a church in Georgia, I met a lovely art major student who told me she wanted to make us a hand painted thirty-foot long silk Menorah (Golden Lampstand). She made it in a gymnasium using many sawhorses. This gorgeous hand painted silk she made we have been using for twenty-seven years. It has three pieces that go together. It is a beautiful labor of love. What a blessing!

God kept putting people in our path He wanted to be a part of this. So many talented and beautiful servants were used to birth this ministry. They all had one pure motive and that was to bring honor and glory to God (*Adonai*).

We built and decorated the succah (booth) each year. As this joyful celebration grew, we had many more people coming to see it. We were blessed to have Yvonne Peters and her dance team who were with us through the early years. Yvonne did some beautiful movements and choreography that we are still doing to this day. Throughout the years, we have had different choreographers take part in this event. Thank you to Chloe Gonzalez, Steve Gonzalez, Bev Pritchard, Hope Dudek, Stephanie Hall, Ellie Potts, and Yvonne Peters. We loved working with all of you. We are still doing some of the dances they choreographed.

Even as I am writing this, I am in awe at how God brought all these artists at different times to add their handprints to His anointed Feast of Tabernacles.

I was the worship leader for the first four years and our worship team was a blessing. Barry's teaching's continued to grow as he grew. Each year, He imparted many nuggets of truth and revelation from the Holy Scriptures to us.

We had silk flags made which were designed by another artist from Tennessee. God brought us a very talented woman, Saundra Reed, who made all of our banners. Each one of them were uniquely designed for our ministry and they are gorgeous. Our Holy banner was designed by a woman in Ohio who gave us permission to copy her banner. This Holy banner is very beautiful and anointed and we use it during the Holy worship segment of our Feast. Another very gifted woman named Karen made our fire flags which we still use to this day.

The thing I love most about this Feast of Tabernacles event is seeing everybody working together in unity to give the Lord our Tabernacle offering. I love seeing the body of Christ, Jew and Gentile, working together for the glory of God. It is a glimpse of the vision of the one new man which is found in the Bible in Ephesians 2:18-19.

Psalm 133:1 says, “How good and how pleasant it is when brethren dwell together in unity.” The Hebrew is: *Hineh ma tov u ma nayim shevet achim gam yachad.*

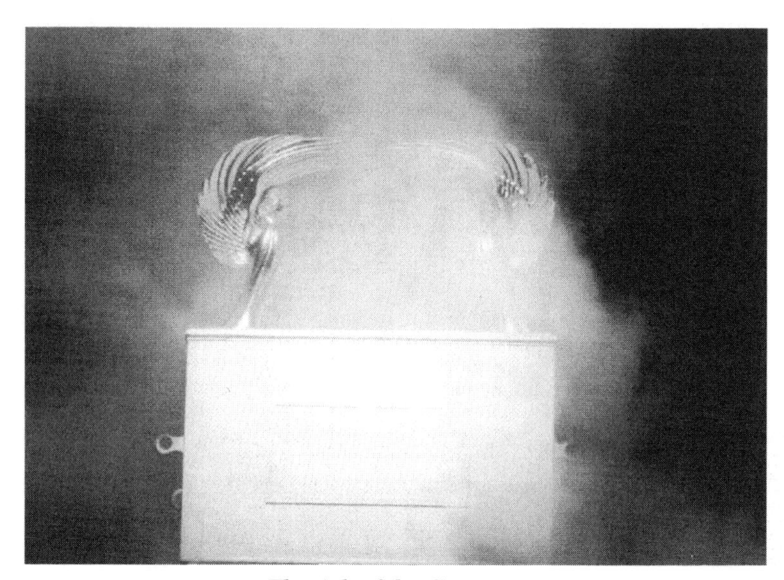

The Ark of the Covenant

The High Priest

Paul Wilbur, worship leader

worship dancers

dancer with wings

Priests with altar of incense

tamborine dancers

Unblemished Offerings

As I have grown in the Lord, I have become acutely aware that God, the maker of Heaven and earth, deserves our very best. I refuse to have a poverty mentality when it comes to anything for the Lord. As we give Him first place in our lives, it will be natural for us to want to give Him our best. Generous giving comes from a heart of thanksgiving. In the Old Testament, the sacrifices the people brought to the temple as offerings to the Lord had to be without spot or blemish. He is Holy and God changes not! We need to learn to bring our unblemished offerings to God.

Let's give God our very best because He is worthy and He is a Holy God, (*Kadosh Adonai*).

After the fourth year of celebrating this Feast, my eyes were opened to the fact that this was looking like a production. To my surprise, my prayer group from Gainesville were right. They had given me a word from the Lord that said, one day I would be doing a production. At the time they shared this with me, I didn't believe it. I said, "I don't know anything about productions." I called my friends and apologized. I told them they needed to come and see this event. They came to our next Feast of Tabernacles and they loved it.

The atmosphere was charged with excitement and joy. The Spirit of God was there. People were singing and dancing and a freedom broke out every year. Each year as the word got out, we had so many people coming from other places who wanted to see this. We decided we had to do this twice. We did it on Saturday evening and again on Sunday morning.

After the Feast was over, some people came to me and said, "If we knew this was so wonderful, we would have brought a bus load of people with us." They did the following year! Year after year this event grew as people began to hear about it.

When the word of the Lord was spoken over me years before, I said I didn't know anything about doing a production. I was looking at my own incapability. What I failed to see was the fact that God knew exactly how to do this. He brought everything and everyone we needed to do this Feast event. I heard a pastor teach once and he said, ***"If the vision is bigger than you, it probably is God."***

The Lord spoke to me and told me that this was the last year we would be doing the Feast of Tabernacles at our church. He did not tell me where we would be going, but He said this was our seventh and final year at our church. There is the number seven again (completion)! This is the year I invited Paul Wilbur, a Messianic artist and worship leader to come and lead us in worship. We were doing many of his songs every year and it made sense to invite him. Paul Wilbur is a beautiful anointed worship leader who was at that time with Integrity Music.

This Feast with Paul Wilbur and his band leading the worship, along with our wonderful dancers and Barry's teaching, made it one of the most powerful and anointed Feasts we had ever done. The Spirit of God showed up and it was beautiful and anointed.

Another artist friend of ours, Karen, came all the way from Ohio. She built a replica of the wall in Jerusalem as the backdrop for this Feast. Can you imagine building this huge wall outside in the heat in Florida? This was a labor of love.

God brings people into our lives for His purposes and when that purpose is done, we may never see them again. Throughout the birthing of this ministry, we have seen how the Lord brings us His chosen ones to accomplish His vision.

We also had a team of young dancers that year who added excitement to the Feast. These dancers were from the Gonzalez family. Their dancing was exquisite, and we thank them for using their gifts for the Lord. The Lord knows who all of you are, and from the depths of our hearts, Barry and I say thank you for making this

Feast of Tabernacles such an anointed worship experience.

Their handprints are all over this Feast and we call them our Feast family. We have been doing this Feast for twenty-eight years, and it is always something we look forward to with great anticipation each year.

The Spirit of the Lord indwells our praises and
He comes and meets with us.
He tabernacles with us.

We Are God's Treasured Possession (Segoulah - Exodus 19:5)

The Lord delights in us and this Feast of Tabernacles is designed by God as a time of meeting with Him. The Hebrew word for meeting is *moedim*. The Lord says these are My Feasts. It is the seventh Feast, in the seventh month, celebrated for seven days. This is the only Feast that is celebrated in the millennium (Zechariah 14). All the nations of the world are commanded by God to come up to Jerusalem every year to worship the King, the Lord Almighty. Those who do not come up will not receive any rain (blessings, prosperity).

This is the final Feast of the biblical calendar year and has the number seven imprinted all over it. It had the greatest number of animal sacrifices of any Feast which was divisible by seven. This was one of three pilgrimage Feasts in Israel. It was called the Feast of Feasts. God's people had to make the journey and come up to Jerusalem to celebrate this Feast and bring their offerings. Jerusalem is the only place that God calls His own. This is where He came to atone for the sins of the world, and this is where He will return to set up His kingdom.

In John 1:14 it says, "The Word became flesh and dwelled among us." The Greek word dwelled is the equivalent of His Shekinah Glory being with them.

Today, God is calling us to come up to a higher place so we can Tabernacle with Him. How awesome is that! The Eternal God, the Great I Am, the One was and is, and is to come wants to meet with us. I pray that we will respond to that call and let go of the things that would keep us from coming closer to Him.

When the Feast celebration with Paul Wilbur was over that night, we met with Paul and his lovely wife because they wanted to talk to us. They said they travel to many different places all over the world and had seen many celebrations, but nothing compares to this. They loved Barry's teaching, the dancers, costumes, and all the artistry that went into this Feast. Then they asked us if we would go with them and do this Feast in their church called New Life in Jacksonville, Florida, and other places. We certainly were not expecting this, but we said yes, it would be an honor. I remembered the word God spoke to me before the Feast. He said, "This was the last year we would be doing this at our church."

I discerned that we were now going with the Wilbur Ministry and God was directing these events. The members of our team were as delighted as we were to do some traveling with Paul. We were the Feast family. We did many Feasts over the coming years, and some other ministry with Paul in different places. There is always such an anointing of God on Paul and his music and our wonderful dancers helped take it to another level. Together we were *Tov*, Hebrew for good. Our vision and calling were the same, so it was a double anointing.

This seventh Feast with Paul Wilbur was the same year some dear friends of ours, Carol and Kit Mason, offered to pay for us to have it videotaped by four professional cameramen. They made this gift to us and we were thankful to be able to capture this worship to God on video. We had to get permission from Integrity Music to make this because Paul was one of their worship leaders. After we had it edited by a professional video man who was a beautiful believer and missionary, we sent a copy to Integrity Music asking them for permission to make it.

The people from Integrity Music called me and told me that this Tabernacle video I sent them was such a professional quality and so beautiful they were all watching it. They said they had never heard such wonderful teaching and asked me who the teacher was. I told them it was my wonderful Messianic husband. They loved the video and gave me permission to put it out. The only restriction they put on it was that I could only use one visual of Paul Wilbur on one song. I also had to get permission from all the other copyright owners to use their music and I had to pay their royalty fees. This entire process from the beginning to the end, took me almost a year. I thank God that He has worked perseverance in me. In 2001, our ministry which is called Hallel Ministries Inc., put out this video to people in our church and locally to other believers. It was a blessing to many people at that time.

A few years ago, I got a call from a woman asking me if I still had that video. I told her that video was very old, and we did not have any of them left. She told me her husband was dying of cancer and all he wanted to watch was that Feast of Tabernacles video. It took him into the presence of God.

She told me he had worn out the one he had. I felt bad that I could not help them, but I did take the opportunity to pray with her. I asked the Lord to give him Peace and take him into His Heavenly Presence.

Trip to Israel with Integrity Music

Paul Wilbur called me one day after our Feast and told me that the Lord told him I was a worshipper. He proceeded to tell me about the Integrity Music tour to Israel. He invited Barry and me to come and join them. My response was I can't think of anyone else I would want to go with. This was going to be a spiritual journey filled with worship. My daughter Susan was very excited about this trip and she decided to go with us. This tour was different than any other tour I have been on. Many of the Integrity Music staff and some worship leaders were on this trip with us. Michael Coleman, the CEO of the company was also there.

One day, we got on two boats and went for a ride on the Sea of Galilee. When we got to the middle of the Sea of Galilee, we turned off the motor and just drifted. The two boats were tied together, and we were one. We worshipped the Lord with Don Moen leading us and it was so anointed and beautiful. There wasn't a dry eye on that boat. This tour was focused on worshipping the

There wasn't a dry eye on that boat.

Lord in all the Holy places. I believe everyone that went on this tour had a spiritual encounter with God.

Another time, we went to see a part of Jerusalem that had been excavated since I was last there. We walked through this area I had never been to and came into a place that had many rows of steps. It reminded me of a large outdoor stadium. When we gathered there, we were told to take our seats on these steps. Don Moen, an anointed Integrity worship leader, started playing his keyboard and he sang a beautiful worship song about the blood of Messiah and suddenly, I started sobbing.

As I was sitting there listening to this music, I realized that we were sitting *on* ***the southern side of the temple, and these were the very steps that the people of God (Israel) walked on in the time of Jesus to come up to the temple*** **to** ***worship God.*** This was the new excavation that they found, and I could see the trough that the actual blood of the sacrifices was poured into. Here we were in this very Holy place and Don Moen was singing about the blood.

I was completely undone, and I could not stop crying. What a spiritually powerful time that was for me. Even now, writing about it reminds me of just how special this place was. To me, these steps to the Temple mount where the Temple was is still Holy ground.

The Treasure Box - A Prophetic Word

We toured many other places in Israel and one day a pastor and his wife from Texas came to Barry and me and told us they wanted a break from touring. They asked if we would take them to Ben Yehuda Street where there were shops and restaurants and we could have some fellowship and lunch together. We gladly accepted and we took them to a place we had been to before called Café Rimon. There was a Messianic believer who played the piano and sang in this café. He was very friendly and talented, and we enjoyed talking to him.

While we were sitting and eating and talking to each other, a tall man walked into the restaurant and came directly over to Barry and me. He told us that he had a word from the Lord for us. He said, ***"God has given you a treasure box, but only as you go and open this treasure box will you receive*** **the treasures."** After this man left, the piano player came over to us and told us that this man was well known in Israel and he was a prophet.

Pastor Sanchez and his lovely wife have a church in Texas. Later, we found out that Pete Sanchez wrote the anointed worship song, "I Exalt Thee." This beautiful worship song went all over the world. The time we spent together was a nice break for us and we really enjoyed spending time with this wonderful couple.

Paul Wilbur did a recording in an auditorium in Jerusalem one night with Integrity Music. This was a very special event that we were all excited to be at. The auditorium was filled with Wilbur fans from all over Israel and they came ready to worship. That was another exciting night of praise and anointed worship.

My daughter and I joined a team of singers on another night to do a musical for the people on our tour. It was called "God With Us." The music was beautiful, and we were thankful that we could be a part of this.

Toward the end of our tour, we went into an old church in Jerusalem called the Church of St. Anne which is known for its remarkable acoustics and reverberating echoes. Paul sang a beautiful song acapella. The anointing of God was so thick it was like one of those high points in your life where you feel a tangible touch from Heaven. He ended with singing the Aaronic Blessing in Hebrew over all of us. I don't believe any of us wanted to leave this place. Thank you, Paul for using your beautiful voice for the Lord and His glory. Barry, Susan and I are so thankful that we made this journey to Israel to worship with you and Integrity Music. It was an unforgettable trip.

The Treasure Box Revealed

Several months after we returned from Israel, I was worshipping God at the piano one morning and it suddenly became so clear to me that ***the treasure box is my piano bench.*** Each time I go to the piano to worship the Lord, I open up the lid of my piano bench to get my music out. My music is inside of the piano bench. The prophet said only as you go and open this treasure box will you receive the treasures. ***The treasures in the box are writing pads full of music the Lord has given me.***

This music He has given me takes me to a place of deeper intimacy with God, the lover of my soul. There is nothing more beautiful than being in God's Presence. Out of my prayer and worship time with the Lord, THE TREASURES COME!

We have been taught to think that treasures are silver, gold, or very precious jewels, but from God's perspective, ***the treasures are our worship***. Every time I go to that piano bench and open it, I sit at the piano and worship Him for hours. At some point in my worship, He gives me a new song. What a revelation, and how beautiful is this, ***that God looks on my worship as a treasure***.

I can hardly grasp what worshipping Him will be like when we are with Him in Heaven and He is seated on His throne. I can find no words for that! Heaven is an entirely different spiritual realm. It's supernatural and we who live on the earth only see in part dimly. Thank You, Lord for the new life You have given me and for filling my very being with so much love and adoration for You. You are glorious in Holiness and I love to worship You. The focus of my ministry and life has been to dwell in a place of worship and present my treasure of worship to you:

"After these things I looked, and behold, a great multitude which no one could number, of all nations, tribes, peoples, and tongues, standing before the throne and before the Lamb, clothed with white robes, with palm branches in their hands, and crying out with a loud voice, saying, "Salvation belongs to our God who sits on the throne, and to the Lamb!" All the angels stood around the throne and the elders and the four living creatures, and fell on their faces before the throne and worshiped God, saying:

"Amen! Blessing and glory and wisdom,
Thanksgiving and honor and power and might,
Be to our God forever and ever.
Amen."

(Revelation 7:9-12)

CHAPTER 13

SPIRITUAL BREAKTHROUGH

Between the years of 1992 and 1999, I felt like I had a blockage in my life because I had no new music. During this same seven years, I was busy birthing the Feast of Tabernacles ministry God had given us. One night, my sister Penny called me from Pennsylvania and told me she had a word from the Lord for me. She said, "Go to your piano, the Lord wants to speak to you." I went to the piano and prayerfully waited for the Lord to speak to me. Suddenly, I was playing a new song He was giving me. It was the first song I had written since my son died in 1992. The song came to me all at once and I loved it.

I was crying throughout this whole process and I felt like walls were crashing down all around me. I was not even aware that I had put up walls to protect myself until that night. After going through so much pain and suffering recently, I suppose I was trying to guard myself from any more hurts. My tears at this point turned into tears of joy. I was spiritually set free that night and He has drawn me closer to Him than I ever was before. What a release and deep inner healing I received that night at the piano. Thank You, Jesus!

After that night, the music flowed out of me and it has never stopped. It was God my Father, who in His great mercy, helped me get back to worshipping Him, the lover of my soul.

I had a meeting with the worship leader of our church and gave him some of the new music I had written. After he had time to go through it, he told me the music was very good and I should make a CD. Barry and I decided to make that CD and our very talented worship leader, Rick Morris, did all the arrangements. We used the Upper Room Recording studio with Tim Kelly who produced it and he was truly a blessing to all of us.

There were a lot of hours of work that went into making this CD and I am thankful to everyone who worked on it. We used many different singers as we recorded the songs. Most of the talented singers were from our church and some were backup singers we hired. The musicians all gave their time and talents to this project and again we say thank you to all who worked on this CD. One of my favorite songs on the CD is called, "Show Us Your Glory." The lead singer, Liz Munizzi, was only sixteen years old when she recorded this. What a great voice God has given her. Another one I love is the title song on the CD called, "My Hiding Place." In times of turmoil and trouble, pain and sorrow, He is **"MY HIDING PLACE."**

Hidden Away - Nashville Recording

Sometimes, we are hidden away for a season or it can be years. It is important during this time to keep moving forward in our relationship with God and in our giftings and calling. A time of being hidden away is not punishment, but quite often God will use it to develop His character in us. It can also be a time of testing because God must see that our obedience and trust is in Him alone. God is shaping us and molding us during these times. God is working in our lives all the time, even when we do not see it. Being hidden away drew me even closer to God. My confidence is in Him and His plan for my life.

Many years ago, I went to Nashville and recorded some of my songs. We did "My Hiding Place" with a new arrangement and producer. Liz Burns, who was Liz Munizzi, is the singer on this song and it is beautiful. She and her husband are pastors of a church in Florida and they have three wonderful children.

Many years ago, I went to Nashville and recorded some of my songs.

We also recorded a powerful song called, "Never Forget You" sung by Chloe Gonzalez. She is also an anointed vessel of the Lord who leads worship in a church in Orlando and has other talents as well. She is married and has three children. That song is about my never ending love for Jerusalem.

The third song we recorded was "Jerusalem." Paul Wilbur was the singer on that song, and it is a very prophetic song. The producing and arrangements for all three of these songs were done by Paul Mills. We greatly appreciate the work he did for us and we are thankful for his God-given gifts. We love the new renditions.

Getting back to the Feasts, our granddaughter, Elizabeth, did a very small part in the Feast with Paul Wilbur when she was only six years old. Every year since then, she has been doing this Feast of Tabernacles with us. The call of God on someone's life can be revealed early on, even though they are but a child. A few years later, we started a junior team of four dancers who were friends of Elizabeth. Our Junior team grew up, and three of them have become part of our core group of dancers in the Feast.

These four young dancers met and had excellent training at the Orlando ballet school. Our granddaughter also got a Bachelor of Fine Arts degree from the University of the Arts in Philadelphia, Pennsylvania. During that time with her busy schedule of classes and rehearsals, she flew home every year so she could dance in the Feast. I can only think of one word, faithful. One of our main dancers Kristen, had her first baby last year in late August. We didn't expect her to be in the Feast. She surprised us and showed up for the first rehearsal one month later. She said she wasn't going to miss the Feast. Faithful.

Our first dance team was also faithful to God as they traveled with us to different churches and events with Paul Wilbur. Many of them paid their own way for the airline tickets and food. We took teams of twelve to sixteen to these different events we were invited to. We traveled to San Antonio, Texas to do an event with Paul Wilbur at Pastor John Hagee's church during Tabernacles. We did another Tabernacles event in a church in Detroit with Paul. We went with Paul to a conference in South Florida that was being held by Jonathan Bernis, Jewish Voice Ministries Int'l. We did many years of Feasts with Paul at his home church called New Life in Jacksonville, Florida. They loved Paul Wilbur's music and we loved worshipping with him. Our junior dance team loved getting to travel with us and it was great training for them to learn to worship God. Overall, it was an exciting time of fellowship and ministry and a great privilege to serve the Wilbur Ministry.

Perseverance and Ministry

One year, I had heart problems and I had to have a heart catherization. Back then, they used extremely heavy sandbags to press on the thigh to stop the bleeding after the procedure was over. I went home and got ready to go do a Feast in Jacksonville at Paul Wilbur's church. The church called me and said, "We heard about your procedure and that you are not coming to do the Feast." I told them that I was coming, but I was going to need a lot of help because I could not lift anything and they said, "We will do everything for you." They were so wonderful. I was black and blue and swollen down one leg, but I refused to let the enemy steal the worship to our God and stop His Feast.

Sometimes, we must be strong and push through the barriers the enemy sets up to stop us. That was a glorious Feast of Tabernacles. Thank You, Lord for all the people You brought to help us. When the body of Christ works together in love and unity, our God loves the offering.

Another time, we were invited to go with Paul to do a Sid Roth conference in South Carolina. Today, his ministry is called, "It's Supernatural." I was in the audience listening to his guest minister that night and it was good. When Paul started to sing and our dancers came running out and danced, a spirit of exuberance and joy broke out.

Sid Roth came running over to me and said, "Thank you for bringing the anointing." It was Paul Wilbur and the dancers who were anointed.

The music was so beautiful, and God's Presence was hovering over us. Sometime towards the end of the evening, someone shouted, "Look up, there is an angel." We all looked up and there was a very large angel standing on the second floor of that conference building. The angel was misty white and had wings, but I only got a glimpse of it and then it was gone. I think you would describe that as a **Sid Roth Supernatural Moment!**

The music was so beautiful, and God's Presence was hovering over us.

The Holy Land - Orlando

In 2002, we did a Feast of Tabernacles at the Holy Land in Orlando, Florida when Marvin Rosenthal owned it. The weather wasn't good due to a tropical storm that moved through. It was lightly raining on and off all day with very windy conditions. We practiced in doors in case the weather didn't clear up. After much prayer, the sun came out and dried the outside seating.

We started the celebration and the seats filled up with people from many different nations. A spirit of joy broke out and it was glorious. At one point in our worship segment, we brought a long red silk cloth which represented the blood of Yeshua (Jesus), coming out of the golden Temple doors. Because of the windy weather, this piece of red silk cloth literally floated in the air by itself coming out of those Golden temple doors! What a sight that was. The dancers who were dressed in nations costumes, took hold of a red silk cloth and carried it down the steps and out through the center aisle.

I was standing in the back watching everything and seeing the response of the people. There was a long row of seats in the back full of young men from South America who had their heads bowed between their legs and they were weeping. Most of the audience were worshipping with us. Paul's music and God's beautiful presence was there that night. Mr. Rosenthal got up after it was over and he was touched. He thanked us for coming and bringing this night of worship to the Holy Land. He immediately opened the auditorium and brought forth the Gospel message for all who wanted to pray and invite Jesus (Yeshua) to come into their lives.

Some of the workers came running over to me and said, "Thank you for bringing the Holy Spirit." They too were in tears. It was a special visitation of God. I am so thankful that even a small celebration moves the heart of God.

The Bible says man looks on the outside, but God looks on the heart. He is the only one who can see the motives of our hearts. Lord, we give You all the honor and glory, for You alone are worthy.

We did Feasts in churches big and small all over Florida. At one church in Lakeland, Florida, we met with the pastoral staff and I started to cry. Their enthusiasm and excitement over this upcoming Feast just touched my heart so deeply. What a heart after God they had. We always brought palm branches and used them in our worship segment. The minute we walked into their main sanctuary I was surprised to see that palm branches were everywhere. They were in the carpet and on some of the walls. This church shouted Tabernacles. The celebration at this church was anointed and they entered in with all their hearts. What a blessing to see the body of Christ rejoice and celebrate God's Feast of Tabernacles. When the Feast was over, a man from Belgium came running over to Barry and me and said, "You two are precious jewels in the hands of God. You have brought Holiness back to the church and God is pleased." He was weeping and was obviously moved by this Feast worship event. We are a royal priesthood and we are here for the purpose of glorifying God.

In 1994, my daughter called to tell me that God told her to get off the mountain in Colorado and move back to Florida. I was totally shocked because she didn't like Florida and loved living in Colorado. She and her husband sold their lovely home and they moved to Florida. They stayed with us for a few months until they bought their new home. We were all going to the same church and doing the Feast and Passover every year. I was babysitting for Elizabeth every day while her parents worked, so we became very close. Now, it was even more obvious to me how Barry's word from God was right on. I was the one taking care of this child, my granddaughter, five days a week. Sometimes, we had a sleepover at our house so her parents could have a date night. She informed me that one day she would be having her own sleepovers with her friends. Little children have a way of bringing laughter and joy to your heart.

The Feast of Tabernacles in Jerusalem

In 1996, I got a call from the worship leader in Jerusalem telling me that this year at their Feast celebration they wanted to do one of the songs I wrote called "Jerusalem." He asked me if I could get him an arrangement for their orchestra as soon as possible. I called a very talented arranger in town and asked him if he would like to do the arrangement. This man of God was so humble he said, "I do not feel worthy." I said, "You are the man." He did the arrangement and wouldn't take any money for it. I prayed many blessings on Terry Winch for years. He and his lovely wife live in the Nashville, Tennessee area and I am sure they are doing well.

My daughter Susan was pregnant with twins during the time we went to Jerusalem to the Feast. Barry was busy working and he could not take time off from work. The Feast of Tabernacles was celebrated each year by the International Christian Embassy in Jerusalem (ICEJ). This was my first time seeing their Feast celebration. It was held every night in an auditorium for seven nights. People from many different nations came to Jerusalem to be a part of this every year. This was very exciting for me to be here and be a very small part of their celebration. I remember the first night I was in the auditorium standing in an aisle near my seat.

A man came running over to me and said, "You are Lana Portnoy." I said, "Yes, I am."

He introduced himself and told me he was the conductor of the orchestra from California. He told me that he loved my song "Jerusalem." He thanked me for the beautiful arrangement I sent, and I told him I was looking forward to hearing it.

We called home many times during that week and Elizabeth would not talk to us. Barry told us she is upset that we went to Jerusalem without her. A few nights later, my daughter stayed back in the hotel because she was tired. I went to the auditorium alone and that was the night they played "Jerusalem." This was the first time I'd heard the beautiful arrangement my friend did. It was so anointed, I just wept! I was sorry that my daughter Susan missed that moment.

The entire Feast was so moving each night and it truly was a spiritual experience for my daughter and me. My favorite part was seeing all of the different nations come up to the city of Jerusalem for seven days to worship God, the Holy One of Israel at this Feast of Tabernacles.

People who came up to Jerusalem from every nation, tribe, and every tongue was like seeing a vision of God's tapestry, a beautiful picture of the body of Messiah Jesus, Yeshua.

When we arrived home, Elizabeth still would not talk to us because we did not take her with us to Jerusalem. She was only three years old, and in her mind, she probably thought Jerusalem was someplace close. Her mother told her that this trip we took to Jerusalem was very far away. We always talked about Jerusalem and her PaPa (grandpa) always played with her about going up to Jerusalem. They would pack her bags and take her dolls and stuffed toys with them and pretend to go up to Jerusalem.

We always played Paul Wilbur's music and danced around the house with her, so she was ready to go. Naturally when we went without her, she felt left behind. The truth is Elizabeth has never been left behind. She has been in every one of our Feasts as a dancer since she was six years old and she has traveled with us to many other places for ministry. However, the one place she has not yet gone to is Jerusalem. We pray that one day in God's timing, the Lord will take her to His beautiful city of Jerusalem.

The Madam Alexander Doll

When my daughter was born in 1962, I bought a Madam Alexander doll of Israel. It was a small collector's doll which was on a shelf for many decades.

Now, we are taking her off the shelf and here is the story.

After traveling to so many places with Paul Wilbur for years, we decided to come home to the Orlando area and do ministry here. One year, we did the Feast of Tabernacles celebration at our large church in Orlando with Paul Wilbur and our Feast family. My daughter, who had not seen our Feast for a few years because we were doing them out of town, called me up and she was crying.

She asked me, "Did I miss my calling?"

I said, "What are you talking about?"

She said, "I saw Elizabeth tonight and I saw the Madam Alexander doll of Israel." ***God was unveiling a spiritual truth that I didn't see until she said it.***

I told her that she had not missed her calling because she was never a dancer and couldn't represent Israel in the Feast. I told her it was her seed, her daughter Elizabeth that God called to represent Israel in the feast. She was the vision of the doll. The doll had dark long hair in braids and blue eyes dressed in an Israeli dress with a star of David around her neck. Elizabeth has long dark hair and blue eyes and she wears the beautiful dress of Israel which has a star of David on it.

Spiritually speaking, this Israel doll I bought in 1962 was a vision God was giving me of something I would be doing forty-five years later with my future granddaughter Elizabeth. How extraordinary is this? The fact that I bought this doll shows the love I had for Israel early in my life.

Fast forward to some forty-five years later. We see the doll dressed in a beautiful Israel dress who is my first-born granddaughter and she is the one dancing in our ministry doing the Feast of Tabernacles. This moment almost took my breath away as I thought about this new insight.

This is so revealing to me that God is past, present, and in the future working in our lives. Dear God, open our eyes to see how You are so present in our lives no matter what we are going through. You are my firm foundation, the rock upon which I stand, and I am in awe of You.

This same Israel costume has been in our feast for many years and was worn by other dancers. I never saw the doll of Israel no matter who wore it. My daughter saw it through her spiritual eyes. Now that it was unveiled, I saw it as well. I saw the vision of the doll in Elizabeth. What a revelation!

I remember one of our dancers came to me when Elizabeth first started to wear that Israel dress and said, "Out of all the dancers who have ever worn that dress in the past, Elizabeth is the anointed one." Even Paul Wilbur's son Nathan told me that Elizabeth is so anointed wearing that Israel dress. He said, "I see beauty and purity and there is an anointing on her to represent Israel."

After I thought about it for a while, I realized that she is the only one who wore that Israel dress who is a Jewish believer. Perhaps that is why she is anointed and carries the mantle for Israel.

You see from this story I am sharing with you that the Lord knew forty-five years later, in my messed-up life, that I would be saved and living a righteous life, and following Him. He knew I would be doing Feasts for Him with Paul Wilbur and He is the one who provided everything in order for us to reach our destiny. He also knew my granddaughter Elizabeth, would become a trained dancer and wear the Israel dress. We are all called and chosen for His purposes.

I said all this to say that God is showing us signs and wonders if we only have eyes to see, and He is involved in our lives even before we are born.

Jeremiah 1:5 says, “Before I formed you in the womb I knew you; before you were born I set you apart.” God has a wonderful and exciting plan for our lives. We have to believe Him and surrender to His will. Let the Holy Spirit lead you in the way you should go. Proverbs 3:5-6 says, “Trust in the Lord with all of heart and lean not unto your own understanding. In all your ways acknowledge Him, and He shall direct your paths.”

I am so thankful for this journey and the opportunities I have had to be a part of so many spiritual experiences in my life. Many people never get to take part in anything beyond their own local church unless they go on mission trips. When you travel and see the Body of Christ in other countries, it expands your vision. We all need to have a fresh revelation from God. Lord, give us wisdom and discernment so that when we see an opportunity to go and do something different, even if it’s out of our comfort zone, we will step out in faith and say yes. I pray You will give us open doors and opportunities to minister locally, and throughout the world.

The call of God is for every believer and not just a few. We all have a calling and destiny to fulfill and God has the plan for each one of us. He will direct our footsteps, guide us, and He will also provide. We have to get past our fears and insecurities and let God direct our lives.

You will be amazed at how much the Lord has for you and you will grow in your giftings and calling as you walk in it. Do not try to figure things out with your mind. God will be your provision and will give you the ticket to go. This will never happen if you do not use the measure of faith which we have all been given. The Bible says without faith, it is impossible to please God.

Persistent, persevering, patient, and Presence-driven faith in Jesus Christ worked out through prayer and continual worship will keep and sustain you through every trial and loss in life.

The Madam Alexander doll of Israel, bought in 1962.

My granddaughter Elizabeth in Israel dress.

CHAPTER 14

THE REST OF THE STORY

The Double Blessing

In concluding this book, I felt you needed to know the rest of this amazing story. I have written about all the loss and death I have experienced in life…but that's not the end of the story. Walking with Christ is filled with the abundant life He gives us. Here's what I testify to…

January 12, 1997, the birth of the twins came about three months after we came home from Israel. They were born very premature and were very small. Our grandson had some serious health problems. He almost died and we had to rush him to the hospital where they gave him blood transfusions. When the twins came home, they had heart monitors on, and these monitors went off every night. The twins were not identical. One was a little girl who they named Emily and she was adorable with red hair. The other twin was a boy, and his name was Zachary. He had dark hair and was very handsome. Elizabeth was looking forward to playing with them, but she soon saw these two newborns were very tiny and it would take time for them to grow. She watched us all taking care of the babies day after day.

One day, she said, "Nana, don't you think that God should have given us one baby at a time? This is just too hard."

She was four years old at the time.

Back in May of 1998, I was on the worship team for the Jubilee celebration. This was the fiftieth-year celebration of the state of Israel that was held at the convention center in Orlando. They had wonderful speakers and Paul Wilbur was one of the worship leaders. I loved Paul Wilbur's music, but at this point, we had only briefly met. Who would have imagined that only two years later, Paul Wilbur would be the worship leader with our ministry doing the Feast of Tabernacles? We have been Tabernacling with God and Paul Wilbur for twenty-one years. We serve an amazing God. What a Blessing Paul has been to us.

My daughter and her husband had been having serious trouble with their marriage for a few years. Her husband never found a job that he really liked, and I don't think he was happy to be living in Florida. My daughter was working for a law firm as a nurse consultant. She lost her nursing career because of her car accident. I advised my daughter and her husband to go for marriage counseling which they did for a long time. They had a beautiful home and children and so much to be thankful for. To make a long story short, they ended up getting divorced and he moved to Atlanta, Georgia. This was the one thing that my daughter never wanted to happen in her life.

Barry and I felt terrible over this breakup happening, and we knew she could not manage on her own working full time and raising three young children. We prayed and felt the Lord would have us move in with her and help her raise the children. We sold our small home without a realtor in one day for cash and moved in with her. I became the cook and chief bottle washer.

The Joys of Grandparenting

Barry and Susan both worked full-time and I stayed home with the children. Looking back on it, I believe the Lord brought us there to be a stabilizing force for Susan and our grandchildren. We celebrated all the holidays, went to church, and we did Shabbat every Friday night. The children loved this and their PaPa (grandfather). There were homecooked meals every day and the children seem to adjust to having us there. The twins were only two years old and couldn't comprehend what happened. Elizabeth was six years old and, of course, it did affect her. She would tell the twins that their dad left and wasn't coming back. They just stared at her because they didn't understand what she was trying to say. I took her aside and gently told her that the twins were only toddlers, and they could not feel the loss that she was feeling.

Elizabeth wanted to audition for the Nutcracker at a dance school where she took a class once a week. They were only taking children who were seven years old, but anyone could audition. I took her for the audition, and she enjoyed seeing all of the other children dance.

A few weeks later, we got a letter in the mail that said they wanted her to be in the Nutcracker which was right before Christmas. Her mother was not happy because she was taking the children to Colorado for the holidays so they could see their grandparents. Elizabeth was ecstatic about being in the Nutcracker and her mother graciously said yes. This was a big boost for Elizabeth because it was a hard year for her in many ways. Her parents got divorced, and she was put back a grade in school, so this was something exciting for her to look forward to. I asked the ballet director why they chose to have her knowing she was only six. They said we took one look at her in the costume and we just had to have her be our youngest child.

Elizabeth blossomed that year because she was in this very professional Nutcracker. The cast all loved her and brought her candy and gifts. The love they all poured on her was quite beautiful. I was worried she couldn't do all the choreography, but the director said by the time the rehearsals are over, she will know everything. She was right, Elizabeth did everything perfect as she was taught and even had an acting part and loved it. We were excited to see her happy about being involved with something that she felt good about. They put on several performances and I was surprised that Elizabeth loved being on stage and wasn't nervous. She was now wanting to be a serious dancer at the ripe age of six. I had no idea at this point that this would become such a big part of her young life. I knew the teacher she had was not good in ballet so I told Elizabeth if she wanted to continue taking dance we would have to go to a different school.

The head of the Orlando Ballet school was Peter Stark. The first day I took Elizabeth to the new school, Peter Stark met us and took one look at her and said she is beautiful. The school called us a few months later and asked if we would allow Elizabeth to be the model for the Nutcracker that year. Her mother said yes. They did a photo shoot with her and the pictures were lovely. They picked the one they liked best and gave us copies of all the pictures. She was on the cover of the Nutcracker program for many years. She was also used for the advertisements in the newspapers and magazines for the nutcracker.

Elizabeth made some friends at the ballet school and she loved having sleep overs with them. Barry and I took turns driving her to ballet classes. Little did we know that two or three of her friends would be dancing with Elizabeth in our Feast of Tabernacles a few years later. Do you see how God is in everything as we follow His lead? These children were all strong dancers and the training they got was excellent. They were in training and little did they know that years later they would dance for God in our Feast of Tabernacles.

Do you see how God is in everything as we follow His lead?

It is so exciting to see how the Lord is at work in our lives. Elizabeth and her friends were in The Orlando Ballet Company Nutcracker with the Orlando Philharmonic for nine or ten years. Fernando Bujones, who was a world-famous ballet dancer, was the wonderful director of the Orlando Ballet Company at that time.

We had many good years with my daughter and the grandchildren. Each child was unique, and we loved them all. Emily was the love of the family. She would greet anyone who came to the house with a big smile and a hug. Zachary and Emily were always close and played with each other. Elizabeth tried to get them to play different parts in the Nutcracker. They would dress up in costumes and she would dance all around them. They soon got tired of this Nutcracker show and went off to play without her. Zachary was always thinking up ways to make money. He would sell homemade tickets for the movie on TV and make popcorn for the audience. Emily has musical gifts and took piano lessons for years. We all went to her piano recitals and she did very well, but after another year went by, she decided to quit. A decision she now regrets.

A woman from our church who was a good Bible teacher came to our house weekly and did a Bible study. I was learning to play the grand piano my daughter had in her house. I did some worship before we started the Bible study. Many women came to the Bible study, and we all grew in the Word. I asked the Lord to teach me how to play the piano enough so I could accompany myself when I did my own music. It was a busy time for all of us and I am so glad that I had a godly husband who would say yes to moving in with them. We lived with them for four years and then I heard the Lord say it was time for my daughter to be the head of this family. The children were older now and in school and we needed to make this transition.

I remember when we sat at the dinner table with them and told them PaPa and I were going to be leaving and moving into a house of our own. Their reaction was funny. My grandson Zachary said, "Oh no, we are all going to starve to death. Who is going to cook for us?" I told them, "Your mother knows how to cook." They all looked at her waiting for her response and she reassured them she could cook.

A Place for His Presence

I went out one day with a realtor friend of mine to look for a house. I told her it had to be big enough for us to have church. I wanted a big family room so we could have people in for worship nights and Bible studies. We have always had groups over to the house to have fellowship and Bible studies. She took me to two houses in Lake Mary which did not have what I needed. Then I said take me back to Longwood and show me what you have there. She took me to a neighborhood in Longwood and we went to see a house that was for sale and had a lock box on it. We walked into the family room and I said, "This is it."

It was the place where we could have church. The family room was huge and had very high ceilings with a lot of windows. She was surprised at how fast I made up my mind. The place was dark, dirty, and dingy looking, but I saw what it could be. After we left, she told me we went to the wrong house. She had made an appointment to see a house which was on the other side of the street. I told her no, the Lord took us to the exact house He chose for us. We bought the house and I spent many months having it cleaned, restored, and we did a lot of updating. This house was now ready to be a place for His presence. The family room holds my grand piano and there is plenty of seating room for people to come. We have been here for seventeen years and we love this house. We have had Bible studies, nights of worship, and fellowship with many different people over the years. I've written many songs that God has given me in this anointed place. It's a peaceful setting that overlooks a pond and we love it. ***The truth is wherever we live is the place for His Presence.*** He lives in us and as we live for Him, His Presence will manifest. We need to develop our awareness of His Presence in our daily life.

It's All about You Lord

I received a phone call from a pastor friend of mine I knew a long time ago. She invited me to come to their church and sing and minister to their women. When I got to the church, I saw that the women were spread out all over the sanctuary. The pastor introduced me. I was sitting at the piano up on the platform. I asked the women who were there to please come closer to me and to each other. I wanted them to experience a closeness with God and each other. They got up and moved to the very front of the room and many of them got up on the platform and sat on the floor all around me. We started with prayer and then went into praise and worship. I sang some of my songs for them and shared parts of my testimony.

They just sat and listened. I could sense the Holy Spirit was hovering over us and I knew the Lord was touching them. Many were crying and there was a sweet presence of God in this place. When I was done and stopped playing, no one moved. There were healings going on with these women and the Spirit of God was moving. It was a special time of intimacy with the lover of their souls, Jesus. The pastor was in tears and she kept thanking me for coming and ministering to these precious ladies. The truth is, I am the one who gets blessed every time I go and pour out to others.

Thank You, Jesus, for using the gifts You have imparted and developed in me for Your honor and glory.

In 2004, my daughter met a man named Steve who she dated for about a year and they got married in 2005. They love to travel and have been to many places all over the world. They have been married for fourteen years now and get along very well. They also play tennis on different teams, so they have that in common. We live very close to one another and do all the holidays together. Susan's children are young adults now and the girls live here in Orlando. Emily graduated from the University of Central Florida in 2019 with a bachelor's degree in psychology and she works at a job in a medical pediatric practice. Zachary, her twin brother lives out in Colorado and loves it there. He is working and learning about the restoration business. Elizabeth graduated with a Bachelor of fine arts degree in dance and she is now living in the

Orlando area with her sister Emily.

In the year 2005, some friends asked us to come to their church and meet their pastor. These friends of ours, Holly and Dennis, came to see our Feast many years ago and fell in love with it. They really wanted to see us bring it to their church. We went to lunch with this pastor and to our surprise he knew about the Feasts of the Lord and loved Paul Wilbur. He was so excited and invited us to come and do the Feast of Tabernacles.

The story is that this is the same Assembly of God church that I went to for years after I got saved. This is the church where many of my family members from Pennsylvania got saved and baptized. This is the same church that Barry and I got married in. I had the strongest feeling that we were being brought here by God, not only to do the Feast, but to be a part of this family of God. My discernment turned out to be right. We did put on the Feast of Tabernacles that year and every year after that. The body of Christ loved the Feast, and some said they waited all year long for us to do it again. It was one of their favorite events.

We became members of this wonderful church and we have been there for fifteen years. We have loved being at this church and enjoyed the Bible studies and fellowship over the years. It seems like we have come full circle back to where it all started. Our church has been a blessing to us and in turn I pray we have also blessed them.

About seven years ago, we got a wonderful dynamic new pastor, Ed Garvin. Pastor Ed was chosen by God to take a struggling church and turn it around and make it into a vibrant church. It is a true picture of the body of Messiah. Many different nations coming together to worship and give God the Glory. He and his lovely wife Jodi came to our Feast of Tabernacles the first year they were here. They sat with us and Pastor told me he was not feeling well and would probably leave early. I was surprised to see him stay until the very end of the Feast. He told me that it was so powerful and beautiful that he couldn't leave. He said in all of his years as a pastor he had never seen anything like it. They loved it.

He told me that it was so powerful and beautiful that he couldn't leave.

Paul Wilbur has done every Feast with us at our church for the past fifteen years. We are thankful to our church for letting us do the Feast every year. When we started there, we had people from other churches in our cast. After the first year, so many young people from our church came to me and asked if they could be a part of it. I loved having them in the Feast and seeing them grow in the Lord each year. We love doing this Feast and our prayer is that this kind of worship will change hearts and draw people closer to God.

This is our Tabernacle offering to God
and we give Him all of the glory, for He alone is worthy.

One year, we did a Passover Seder for the Women of the Word Bible study group the year that Jane was teaching us. Sandra Joseph and I put it together and my husband did the teaching. The elders and their wives came, and it was an anointed time of teaching, music, and good food. The young servers came and joined us and afterwards they told me how much they learned from my husband Barry. Our new pastor and his wife came that night and they, too, were pleased to see us doing this Passover Feast. We tied it into the last supper that Jesus had with His disciples and we ended it with taking Holy Communion. Our ladies from our Bible study all made food and I brought all the elements for the Passover.

At the end of the night, our pastor said, "Isn't it wonderful that we have Dr. Barry and Lana who can lead us and enlighten us in learning more about this Passover Feast."

I personally think we see the bigger picture when we put the Old Testament and the New together. After I came to the Lord, I was astounded at how much of the Old Testament was connected to understanding the New. The Word of God from the first page of Genesis to the last page in Revelation is all inspired by God.

Romans 11 tells us that God's plan of salvation from the beginning was that the whole world would be saved through Jesus, Yeshua. The Messiah came for His own and as a nation they rejected Him. The Lord knew that they would reject Him and He allowed a partial blindness to happen to Israel until the fullness of the Gentiles has come in. Salvation has come to the Gentiles to provoke Israel to jealousy. If their rejection is the reconciliation of the world, what will their acceptance be but life from the dead?

All Israel will be saved. As it is written, the deliverer will come from Zion (*Yeshua*) who will turn godlessness away from Jacob. And this is my Covenant with Israel when I take away their sins.

The Lord spoke to my husband and I this year and told us it is time to write the book. We got a publisher and hired a ghost writer who I thought would write the book. The ghost writer told me that I had to write the book and he would coach me and do some editing throughout the process. He told me it had to be my voice telling the story. This made perfect sense to me, but it wasn't what I wanted to hear. God must have a sense of humor because here I am writing the book. This has been one of the hardest things I have ever done. At the same time, it has brought me great joy and more inner healings that I didn't even know I needed. God knows us intimately and He knows what we need even when we don't. The depth of His love for us is more than we can comprehend.

I want to say thankyou to my ghost writer Dr. Larry Keefauver for encouraging me to write the book. I love your sensitivity and thank you for the patience you had with me. I am very grateful for all the help you have given me even though I am not always on the same page as you are. Barry and I thank God that He brought you into our lives at this very time to help us accomplish this God ordained book. May the Holy One of Israel bless you and your family with good health, love, and prosperity in all that you do.

Barry and I also want to say thank you to David Welday, Michelle Buckley, and his staff at Higher Life Publishing Co. He encouraged me to tell my testimony and agreed that it would help people who are going through difficulties in their own lives. The times that we are now living in are full of stress and anxiety like we have never seen before. May this testimony book help them to see their need for God.

Because of God's Faithfulness, We Stand Victorious

I would like to say thank you to my loving husband Barry, who has also been my spiritual partner and best friend for over thirty-two years. I can honestly say they have been the best years of my life. We have come through so much together, battles that would have torn any marriage apart. Because of God's faithfulness, we have come through victorious! We have never stopped loving and honoring each other. The Lord knitted us together in a beautiful way for His purposes, and we answered that call together. **God is the best match maker!** He brought me my rabbi, a man of the Word.

You have shown the Father's love and have brought healings to our children and to our precious grandchildren. I am thankful for your daughter Denisha who got saved in college, and to her husband Phil for their love and prayers over the years. We love our grandchildren Rachel and Isaac who are grown up and living in Florida. Dear Barry, you are loved more than you will ever know. God knew what a match we would be, and I am thankful He chose you to be the husband for me. You are brilliant in your teachings in the Feasts year after year, and I am proud of the man of God you have become. You are highly respected by your colleagues in the medical field and you have helped so many people along the way who needed your medical skills, knowledge, love and compassion.

Thank you for your encouragement and prayers with me writing this book.

I have laid my soul bare in this book, hoping that it will help people who are going through difficult times in their own lives. I have shed tears that I didn't know were there. Life is often not fair, and sometimes there is no justice, but I can't imagine going through life without God. He gives me strength when I have no strength. He gives me peace in the midst of uncertainty, chaos and turmoil. His unconditional love is like no other. God is faithful and steadfast, loving and compassionate, Holy and righteous and I choose Him. My prayer is that people will glean from our mistakes and messed up lives and see, the only answer for any of us is to give our lives to the God of Abraham, Isaac, and Jacob. Jesus, Yeshua, is the only one who can save us, and forgive all our sins.

The problem with the world is a sin problem, and only Jesus can change that.

I pray for all who read this book that they will be seekers of truth. I hope you have seen the thread of the faithfulness of God woven throughout the story of my life. My search is over; for me to live is Christ. ***Life is all about choices, and the choices that we make will determine our destiny, in this life and* ETERNALLY!**

JESUS IS THE MISSING PIECE.

ACKNOWLEDGMENTS
HEARTS OF GRATITUDE FROM BARRY AND LANA

Thank you to the Paul Wilbur Ministries International

Over the course of many years, Barry and I have spent time with the Wilbur family and gotten to know them well. We love and respect them for who they are and for how they live their lives for God. We love their family and have prayed for them over the years. Thank you to Nathan and his lovely wife Malki. You have always been there to help your Dad and us. Working with you has been a real joy. Give Caleb your precious son a hug from us. We send our love to Shae and Joel and the newest baby, Shiloh. We are happy for you and rejoice in all that you have accomplished in your young lives. Your newest CD is very powerful, Shae and

I love it. Keep on singing and writing for our Messiah, the best is yet to come. Thank you to Paul and his beautiful wife Luanne, who were very good to us and encouraged us as we walked through some difficult times in the early years. Luanne, you are such a faithful prayer warrior and so dedicated to your family and the ministry. You are truly a Proverbs 31 woman. We love you and Paul and thank you for all the opportunities you gave us to go and minister with you. Today, your ministry is all over the world, but still you remain the same loving Godly people.

It has been the highlight of our lives to serve this man of God, Paul Wilbur. This year will be our twenty-ninth year in ministry of celebrating The Feast of Tabernacles and Passovers in many places. We have been with Paul Wilbur twenty-one of those years. We pray unlimited showers of blessings over the Wilbur ministry. May you have many more productive years to cover the earth with your anointed worship and prophetic ministry. You are family to us, and we love you all dearly. Thank you, Paul, for recording "Jerusalem" in Nashville for us and may the Lord use it in these uncertain prophetic times we are living in. As the world gets darker, God's light shines brighter. Thank you for choosing us so many years ago. We are honored and always feel blessed to minister with you.

Thank You, Lord, for all who have given of themselves to serve and work with us in this ministry over all these years. We have had faithful servants who take time off from work and come to our house to pack our trucks with the Feast props and costumes year after year. After the Feast is over and the people go home, our team of men pack the trucks once again and we all work until very late in the night putting everything back in storage. Thank you, Ken, Richard, and Brent who not only pack trucks, but also run around with flags during our Feast. These same men and Charles are also our priests in the worship segment. You are special to us and to God.

To Charles and Susan who have been with us for so many years, we love you and thank you for your love and encouragement to us throughout the years. Thank you, Terry and Dee, for being such a part of these Feasts for so long. Terry, your drama part is so touching, and you do it with such a heart of God. We remember all the years you both were in the Feast, but also stayed and helped us clean up and pack our trucks. We love you and ask the Lord to take care of you and bless you.

Thank you, to the Calvary technical team and the media team from our church who do such a great job every year setting up the stage and doing the sound and lighting. Thank you also to Nancy Alford who arranges the rehearsals and room schedules for us every year. Good job and we love you Nancy. It takes a team of many to bring forth this event.

I want to say a special thank you to my sister, Penny and her husband Rick, who come from Pennsylvania each year to help us with this Feast. Penny has come early to help me organize all the costumes and props and she helps with costumes and the clean up after the Feast is over. We also want to thank Penny and our dear friends Carol and Richard who have served us by decorating the succah every year. You are the artistic servants of the Lord and you are loved.

My daughter Susan and her husband Steve also help us each year. They run errands to pick up food for the Wilbur ministry and us. They also stay and help us clean up afterwards and help organize everything that has to be put back on the trucks. We thank you for all your help and may the Lord reward you for serving.

I want to also thank Mindy Napier, who for years helped with the wardrobe costuming part of our Feast. Thanks, Mindy, for traveling to some of the places in Florida with us when the girls were so young. I remember how you spoiled them and gave them candy and sodas and they were bouncing on the beds. Hope you got some sleep! Thank you Melinda Howard, Cheryl Scotti, and Jan Bruggerman. These lovely ladies work at our ministry table each year. You always do such a wonderful job of representing our Hallel Ministry. We appreciate all you do for the Lord and His glory. Blessing on you all in Yeshua's name.

A big thank you to Debbie Boutin for being in our core dance group for so many years and also doing rehearsals with the cast. We pray blessings on you and Paul and your whole family.

Thank you to Linda Welker who also danced in our group for so many years. We are blessed to have you doing the rehearsals with the cast in recent years and we all love you. Linda, you are a beautiful heavenly picture when you worship with those golden wings.

Thanks to Rick and Jeff Welker who provide us with gorgeous palms we use for the succah decorations and to worship our Lord. Your faithfulness to the Lord is outstanding. Twenty- eight years you have provided us with beautiful palms.

We thank Theresa McIntire, who year in and year out sewed costumes for us, and also danced with our core team.

A very special thank you to Claude and Freeda Bowers, who are friends of ours. We thank you for all the television spots on WACX you have given us for all these years. You have been there every year helping us promote this beautiful Feast of the Lord. We love and appreciate all that you do for the kingdom of God. May the windows of heaven open up for you with blessings you cannot contain. Prosperity in your ministry, health, and family. I pray the Majesty building will be finished and used for its God-given purpose and for the glory of God in Jesus mighty name.

Thank you to the young dancers who grew up watching the older woman dance and worship the Lord. They have mentored you and you have grown into a wonderful team of worshippers and have been so faithful for so many years. It's a blessing for us to see your enthusiasm and love for this Feast ministry year after year.

We also thank the men who have been servants and helped us for some twenty some years. We love you and it truly blesses us to see you put such a high priority on this Feast every year.

Thank you to Victoria Marluando who has danced with us now for many years. You are beautiful inside and out Victoria, and we love having you.

Allison you are a treasure to us as a dancer and as a friend. You come all the way from St. Petersburg for all the rehearsals and the performance. Faithful.

Michelle you are also very special to us. You have been with us since your childhood. You are also faithful.

There are so many other dancers that we thank for being a part of us and for giving your gifts and talents to be used for the Lord. Thank you, to all the dancers who ever danced with us:Yvonne Peters, Alex Rodgriguez, Judy Wagner, Debby Yero, Linda Welker, Jan Huttinger, Donna Nichols, Debby Beynon, Cindi McDaniels, Debby Boutin,Theresa McIntire, Lin Giard, Elizabeth Bernstein, Kristen Kozy, Victoria Marluando, Allison Meleen, Erin Pritchard, Michelle Meyer, and Simone and Charlotte Marmol. I know that I have missed some who were with us in the early years and I am very sorry. You know who you are, and I thank you for your participation.

A special thank you to Kim Beveridge, who designs beautiful dance costumes and came from Ohio with her dance team one year to help us out. We miss you and love you Kim.

Barry and I want to especially say thank you to our shofar player, Pastor Bill Sharp. This is a man of God who comes to our Feast every year and blows the shofar for us. Faithful!

We thank all of you who are our Feast family and are a part of the cast each year. The children who grew up doing this feast and are now adults in the Feast. You participate because of your love for the Lord and we love having you be a part of this glorious celebration.

A special thank you to our photographer, Tim Kelly who has come and taken great pictures every year. It is hard to take photos of moving targcts (dancers), but we have some wonderful pictures of them and all the cast. Thank you also for designing our posters every year. You have been a long-time personal friend of ours and we love you and your wife Laura.

We want to thank each and every young person who have been in this Feast over the years. There are far too many for me to name, but God knows you and we want you to know we love and appreciate you. You are all precious in God's eyes.

Last but certainly not least, we want to say a special thank you to our daughter Susan, who has been with me and encouraged me throughout my life. She has served us in different ways and given to our ministry for many years. I pray the Lord will give you the desires of your heart as you continue to seek Him in all that you do. You have encouraged me whether I'm writing music or doing the Feasts of the Lord. Barry and I love you and thank you for all you have done throughout the years. Thank you for giving us three wonderful grandchildren. You are the soul winner of the family, and that is the most important calling.

ENDNOTES

1 Proverbs 22:6 NKJV, Proverbs 13:22

2 Romans 8:28

3 Religious Jewish children learn this passage from Deuteronomy 6:4-5 which is called *The Shema.* The Shema is one of only two prayers that are specifically commanded in Torah (the other is Birkat Ha-Mazon -- grace after meals). It is the oldest fixed daily prayer in Judaism, recited morning and night since ancient times. It consists of three biblical passages, two of which specifically say to speak of these things "when you lie down and when you rise up." This commandment is fulfilled by including the Shema in the liturgy for Ma'ariv (evening services) and Shacharit (morning services). Traditional prayer books also include a Bedtime Shema, a series of passages including the Shema to be read at home before going to bed at night. (http://www.jewfaq.org/shemaref.htm)

4 Deuteronomy 6:6-9 MSG

5 https://www.brainyquote.com

6 John 4:25

7 See John 1:10-11

8 See Proverbs 19:21

9 See Lamentations 3:22-23

10 See 2 Corinthians 5:17

11 John 3:5 and 3:16 from the *Tree of Life Version* (TLV) Tree of Life Translation of the Bible. Copyright © 2015 by The Messianic Jewish Family Bible Society.

12 Matthew 4:19 TLV

13 *Spirit Tales Spirit Tale One: The Wheelwork: Don't You Know You're Not Alone!*

14 https://tinyurl.com/y2qvdqmy

15 Lucado, Max. *Grace for the Moment: Inspirational Thoughts* Nashville: Thomas Nelson, p.3.

16 See Proverbs 3:5-6

17 See Revelation 19

18 Orlando Sentinel, February 14, 1987

19 Exodus 33:14-15

20 John 16:13 TLV

21 Isaiah 40:30-31 TLV

22 Proverbs 3:5 and 16:20 (AMP)

23 Ephesians 3:20 from The Passion Translation (TPT) The Passion Translation®. Copyright © 2017 by BroadStreet Publishing® Group, LLC. Used by permission. All rights reserved. thePassionTranslation.com

24 Romans 8:28

25 See John 10:10

IF YOU'RE A FAN OF THIS BOOK, WILL YOU HELP ME SPREAD THE WORD?

There are several ways you can help me get the word out about the message of this book...

- Post a 5-Star review on Amazon.
- Write about the book on your Facebook, Twitter, Instagram – any social media you regularly use!
- If you blog, consider referencing the book, sharing my website.
- Recommend the book to friends – word-of-mouth is still the most effective form of advertising.
- Purchase additional copies to give away as gifts.

The best way to connect with me is visiting my website

www.LanaPortnoy.com

The Missing Piece is available at these fine retailers